D0876596

RA PRESS
100 Kennedy Drive #53
South Burlington, VT 05403

Grateful acknowledgement is made to The Literary Gazette where the chapter Waterfalls first appeared. Also, thanks is due to Barbara Louise Ungar for her insightful editorial suggestions, and to Susan Dann Leslie for her proofreading help.

Photo Credits: front and back cover: Fay Bartow

Book Design: Sean Tierney

Copyright 2014
all rights reserved
www.rapressrafilms.com

ISBN   978-1-312-56429-9

TEACHING TROUT TO TALK

The Zen of Small Stream Fly Fishing

Stuart Bartow

All fish are mute..., one used to think.   But who knows?
Isn't there at last a place where, without them, we would be able
to speak in the language of fish?   Rainer Maria Rilke, *Sonnets to Orpheus, Part II, XX*

Upon what do the fowl of the air meditate?   Upon what do the fish in the water meditate?   They fly; they swim.   Is that not enough?...Zen ought to be lived as a bird flies through the air or as a fish swims in the water...The idea of Zen is to catch life as it flows.

"Within Joshu's cup of tea the mermaids are dancing."   So long as one is conscious of space and time, Zen will keep a respectable distance from you.

Zen must be seized with bare hands, with no gloves on.
D. T. Suzuki

Man, living in the dust,
Is like a bug trapped in a bowl.
All day he scrabbles round and round,
But never escapes from the bowl that holds him.
The immortals are beyond his reach,
His cravings have no end,
While months and years flow by like a river
Until, in an instant, he has grown old.   HAN-SHAN

To all the Marcos of the world who fish in pools large or small, like McElligot's, dreaming of magical fish teeming beneath their waters, and to Izaak, a boy who likes to fish and spells his name the same as the author of The Compleat Angler.

Author's Note:

This is not a linear book. Though this book reads perfectly well (I hope) sequentially from page one until the end, readers can also pick chapters randomly, if they prefer, with no diminishment, as far as I can tell, of the reading experience.

Author's Second Note:

This book took approximately seven years to complete. However, I did not spend seven years writing it. This book would have been finished sooner, but its completion got in the way of my fishing.

CONTENTS

11

Prologue

I went out to the hazel wood,
Because a fire was in my head,
And cut and peeled a hazel wand,
And hooked a berry to a thread;
And when white moths were on the wing,
And moth-like stars were flickering out,
I dropped the berry in a stream
And caught a little silver trout.

W. B. Yeats, *The Song of Wandering Aengus*

I began fly fishing not because there was a fire in my brain, but because of longing, a primeval nostalgia for something I had never done before. I was also homesick. Homesick for the water. I missed the sea. But I was, and still am, far from the ocean, living near the Vermont border in upstate New York. Life's duties and emotional ties kept me from simply moving near the coast. But it so happened that I lived close to some of the most legendary fly fishing streams in the world, including the Battenkill and Mettawee Rivers. *When there is no ocean nearby, a pond will do.* Wading into these rivers, and the many small streams that either feed them or run near them never cured me of my sea fever, nothing can do that, but in them I discovered another beauty, perhaps more subtle, but equally enchanting. Yet why did I take up fly fishing, the most arcane type of angling? I could simply have returned to fishing in ponds and lakes, as I had done on and off since a boy, with a spinning rod. I suppose I wanted a challenge. I suppose I am an over-achiever. Maybe I secretly envied the elegance of the fly cast. Maybe I wanted to find out for myself just what it was that made one speak of fly fishing as though of some holy activity or practiced benediction. Perhaps I needed to learn just what it was, exactly, that I had shunned so long as an effete activity. Maybe it all began with a painting I often marveled at as a child. My uncle had over his mantle a large oil painting of a fly fisher in a trout stream. If you looked closely at the picture you could see the fisher was my uncle. The painter had cleverly captured his image. (*How did my uncle get in the picture?*) I now know that working a portrait into a painting isn't impossible for a good artist, but the sense of mystification that painting gave me remains, as though it were a magic portal. Not only had my uncle's image been miraculously transposed into the picture, but the setting itself was forbidding. The stream was rocky with surging riffles; the trees in the background were dark, primeval. The fact of the fisher in the middle of this wild place fascinated me. How could one enter such a haunted and dangerous place, inaccessible to a five-year-old and, of all things, be fishing there?

What else made me take up a fly rod? Was it the lore and literature? I doubt that. I had heard that for true fly fishers, making a good cast is as important as catching a fish. I now realize this is not really true, that actually the two are together, seamless, yet I was intrigued that to be good at this type of angling didn't require catching fish, that catching fish was ancillary to being skilled at the art of the fly. Reference to fly angling as an art rather than a sport had much to do with my eventual surrender to fly fishing. What makes it an art? I knew that this was one art form that had to be practiced to be understood. It couldn't be learned through a book. Maybe, after all, the fish had lured me, those wild and elegant little beings so different from us, stubbornly unknowable, survivors of the Ice Age with an ancestry going back scores of millions of years. Yet, why fly fish? Why not fish the usual, easier way with a spinner rod and reel? I am not entirely convinced that you can catch more fish with a fly rod than spinner fishing. I am convinced of this, however: that it's simply more fun, more exciting to catch a fish with a fly rod. There is less machinery between you and the fish when playing a fish on a fly rod.

One of the purposes of this book is to demystify those aspects of fly fishing that exclude people from this practice. Fly fishing itself can never be demystified because, the better one gets, the more magical it becomes. Yet there are fundamental qualities of fly fishing that have entered the domain of esoterica that really aren't so mysterious after all. I suspect that over the years many fly fishers themselves have been responsible for embellishing the arcana of fly fishing, perhaps to keep pretenders away, perhaps because, like some of the Zen hermits of ancient days, we find it humorous to write a 100-page tome on how to properly tie one's shoes, and even more humorous that someone would read such a book.

The past couple decades or so there has been a change in what was once perceived as an elitist sport for only the most skillful (and wealthy) of anglers. Many fly fishers themselves now seem dedicated to debunking those forbidding aspects of the practice in order to get more people interested, and are conducting instructional classes often at night and on weekends, frequently volunteering their knowledge all year round. With increased gentrification of wild locales and pressure to develop areas near our most beloved trout streams, an effective way to inspire people to conservation and environmentalism is to make them one of us. There is no one who will be more dedicated to preserving a trout stream than a fly angler. Any Zen fly fisher will tell you, it's not simply about catching a fish, but fly angling is a particular way of experiencing the stream one is in, experiencing the inside and outside -- let's say erasing the inside and the outside of the moment one is in. I am not certain this book will make anyone better at fly fishing in that they might catch more fish. Yet, my hope is that this work enhances the angler's chances at having a better overall experience.

There are a couple disclaimers I should make at the start. This book is not the *place* to learn Zen, that most simple yet elusive practice of the spiritual life. The best introductions to Zen for English readers can be found in the works of the Japanese scholar D.T. Suzuki and the American philosopher Alan Watts. This book is a good place (I don't know if a book is a place; it is a crystallization, or space that opens when one gets inside like a stream) to discover the parallels and affinities to be found between fly angling and Zen. It should go without saying that the best way to learn fly fishing is to go fly fishing, after someone experienced has shown you the basics of casting, fly selection, knot tying, and fish location.

KOANS

If you fish where there are no fish, are you still fishing?

You can catch the right fish with the wrong fly, but you can never catch the wrong fish with the right fly.

If you cast your fly upstream and it quickly returns between your legs, and no one witnesses this, do you still look foolish?

You may catch a bat when fly fishing, but you will never have him mounted.

How do you mount the fish that got away?

How do you stop the fighting across the river?

If a trout is taken by an osprey before the fisher has landed it, should the fisher let go of his fly rod, or risk being taken to another part of the river?

If you fish dry fly, can you catch a dry fish?

Casting upstream, the fly returns and snags you. When you unsnag the fly that has you, are you caught and released?

If you cast no shadow in the world of humans, people may avoid you. If you cast no shadow in the stream, fish won't flee you.

If you lie about fish you didn't catch, do you accumulate bad karma?

Do fish have souls, or are they souls?

The Three Stages of Fly Anglers

Trout are in the Salmonidae family of fish, which means they are powerful, even when young, and can swim upstream as rapidly as downstream. They fly through the water so fast that when one darts by, you think perhaps it was a trick of the eye or the shadow of a bird flicking past. This fact remains true whether you are in a small stream or a storied trout river, whether the trout you are casting for are lunkers or younger fish. Why this is significant to me is that you can have a challenging experience, albeit on a much smaller scale, when fishing in brooks and creeks, in many ways even more challenging than on large rivers.

George W. Harvey, in his book *Techniques of Trout Fishing and Fly Tying*, describes trout anglers as going through three stages. In the early stage, the fisher wants to catch the limit, as many fish as possible. After a while, this loses its luster and the fisher wants to catch large trout, perhaps takes up night fishing when the likelihood of catching big fish is greater. In the final stage we find the angler fishing like a hermit in the mountain brooks where the wild fish are, where there is solitude, where breed new challenges and the fly fisher makes discoveries about trout and must be innovative in discovering them. Angling in these out-of-the-way streams makes the angler more conscious about conservation, more inclined to catch and release, and fiercer in the desire to protect these havens of wildness.

The Why of Small Streams

The water called me. I decided to pay attention to what was near, and when I did I saw trout streams. The part of the country where I live, inside the valleys between the Green and Taconic Mountains, is richly veined with trout streams, many of which, though threatened, are abundant in wild trout. Although I began fly fishing in the bigger, more well known rivers, I gradually drifted to small streams, which I had initially shunned as too difficult to fish in, or unlikely to bear many trout. The streams have a primeval beauty that the bigger trout rivers lack. With increasing use and development along their banks, wild fish populations along rivers like the Battenkill are severely stressed in ways small streams are not, though only one misguided development project can put a small stream in peril, vulnerable to disappearance in ways that larger streams are not.

The creeks, brooks, and small rivers offer an intimacy, a solitude that larger rivers can't provide. They are also tricky. The fish are more easily spooked. In order to avoid catching everything around except a trout, casts must be short and precise. I recommend learning to fly fish on streams large enough so that you can practice all types of casting, because the precise casting one needs on small streams takes some practice to develop. Even the most skillful fly fisher gets line tangled in an over-hanging branch or in the grass along the bank. If he never does, he's being far too careful to ever make a genuinely elegant cast. You simply have to accept the reality that you are going to catch bushes and branches now and then. To fish in a stream where no one ever fishes, or hasn't fished in years, for trout that are streamlined and strong, born of the waters in which they live, trout that have never in their lives seen a dry fly drop in the water above them, is the joy of small stream fishing. Every now and then you will make a precision cast into a translucent spring pool, and witness the trout as it streaks through the water to take your floating caddis fly. I won't pretend that this kind of fishing is for everyone. Some agility and balance is necessary, including a desire to reach places that may be barricaded with thorns, and rife with noxious plants and insects. But for me, it's worth the trouble to get at the wild, undisturbed fish, to wear old jeans and sneakers so I don't have to worry about tearing expensive waders on a wild rose bush. To be in the place where dragonflies zigzag around you, and the machinery of the highway is distant, you may have to haul yourself through grape vines, raspberry canes, stinging nettle, poison ivy, while horseflies and deer flies regard you as food. But maybe you are like me, and can forget about the bites and scratches once in the stream.

The Fly Fishing Master

A monk once went to Gensha, and wanted to learn where the entrance to the path of truth was. Gensha asked him, "Do you hear the murmuring of the brook?" "Yes, I hear it," answered the monk. "There is the entrance," the master instructed him. From Carl Jung's foreword to D.T. Suzuki's *An Introduction to Zen Buddhism.*

How do you know when you've met a fly fishing master, or, better yet, when do you know that you have arrived? In other words, when can you realistically say you are good at fly fishing? Simple.When you catch trout consistently and have fun doing so. Yet this simple answer does require examination. If you have fun only when you catch a fish, playing and landing it, then you are not *good* at fly fishing. Most of the time a person is fly fishing, or during most other types of fishing, the fisher is not catching fish, which opens up the fisher to other things. (I do not include commercial trawling here, which isn't fishing. Commercial trawling is sea plunder.) Most of the time when fly fishing, nothing is going on. Or everything is.

The Red-winged Blackbirds are squabbling in the dense brush along the stream bank. Killdeer streak low over the waves. Dragonflies are making strikes on the surface that leave circles on the water the size of dinner plates. The sunlight blades its white fire on the surface of the stream. Thoughts and memories go and come and go again, and happiness, which is good for the heart, spreads about you in a field, a stream of energy. There is too much suffering in the world. Yet one person's joy, I believe, can counter, if only in a small way, suffering, including the suffering of others. I am not talking about some televangelist expounding on the goodness of being wealthy as sign of God's grace, but of allowing oneself to interpret birdsong as joyful. Opening up. Self-absorption is psychic poison. Being in a river, as long as you don't drown, is an effective counter to self-absorption. As far as I know, Dante never fished, but it's no coincidence that he reserved a special place in hell for the sullen, those who willfully reject what is beautiful in life, who purposely close themselves to that which is freely given to all. As the sullen can poison those who come in contact with them, joy can be as contagious as sorrow. It doesn't matter how many fish you catch. I would argue that if you don't feel a sense of joy, or

24

connect with the energy stream you are in while fly fishing, then you really are not any good at the practice. For some decades now in American and western culture, much has been made of the elusive experience named "transcendence." Literary interest goes back even farther, with Thoreau and Emerson advocating direct communion with Nature, nature with a capital "N." When I play and land a trout fly angling, the exhilaration must be akin to what we call transcendence, temporary or not. The joy lies in the entire experience that culminates in the physical pleasure of seeing a secret beauty, then freeing it, which leaves me beaming long after the encounter. Transcendence is not in killing the fish, but its coming near to death at which point in space and time the fish and fisher connect, something Hemingway often reached for in his prose. The problem with Hemingway may be the suggestion that such a connection can happen only with leviathans. Let's face the fact that it's hard to tell compelling fish stories about little fish.

Does the fish transcend? Doubtful. But I believe the fly angler "goes somewhere" else through closely feeling, then beholding, momentarily, this living, spangled presence whose life is profoundly threatened, whose experience of reality does not include the fisher. Often an artist's response when asked what their favorite piece or work is, is "The next one." Though I understand the faith behind this response, I believe there is a better response when asked what one's favorite catch is. My response would be, "The one that is on right now."

It is precisely the fact that most of the time the fly fisher isn't catching any fish that gives all the drama and excitement to the moments when the fisher does have a fish on. If a fisherman goes out, for example, for four hours and catches one trout, whether early, middle, or late during the adventure, that fisher has had a good day. Four hours outside on a lush morning, spent standing or wandering in a trout stream, with a 9 inch brown trout caught and released, is a superb trip. If someone goes out for four hours, catches eight 14 inch browns, but rues the one that got away or wishes he had caught more, he may be great at catching fish, but he is not good at fishing. So the answer is both simple and complex. When you are accomplished at fly fishing, you simply know it in the same way a violinist knows her art form, or a baseball player knows when he is a good hitter. You are a fly fishing master when you catch fish consistently and when you experience joy consistently.

Spells and Casting

Something few fishers will tell you is that you will eventually develop your own style of casting. Many of those who have written books on fly angling or who teach the art leave novices with the impression that in the classic style of casting (the 10:00 o'clock—2:00 o'clock arc) any deviation from that style is sacrilege.   An expert fly fisherman once told me, like a baseball batting stance, it's not so much how you begin, but how you finish, or how the cast ends in the water.

Begin by having someone who knows how to cast show you. Afterwards, casting well is simply a matter of practice.   There is no need to make classic, thirty-foot casts all the time.   A good twenty-foot cast will often do in larger streams, and sometimes overhanging shrubs or trees might cause you to make sidearm or roll casts, a technique I like, often prefer, even in open water when a roll cast can land your fly perfectly in pools or riffles that are under low hanging willows, branches or shrubs. Being primarily self-taught, I started roll casting without knowing that what I was doing had a name. (I learned the name was roll casting by hanging out with some Trout Unlimited guys during a highway cleanup.) Roll casting is best in tight places in which you use very little, sometimes just leader and tippet, and flick the fly rod with your wrist, allowing the line to arc over your shoulder.   Keep in mind that your casts won't be balanced unless you use the right weight fishing line for your fly rod, the right sized leader for the line, and the right sized flies for your leader line.   The words to repeat are *soft and delicate*. Nice and easy.   A good cast occurs when your line hits the water before your fly.   A good cast isn't forced.   *Casts like ghosts whispering over and behind you*.   Remember also that you don't need to make perfect casts to catch fish.

Other fly fishers might disagree, but I suggest learning to cast with your opposite hand, or learning with either hand. When I first learned I took the fly rod instinctively in my right hand (I'm left handed). There just seemed to be too much will and strength in my left.   My right side felt more open, child-like, malleable, ready to be taught gracefulness. Admittedly, I have become somewhat ambidextrous over the years, which I believe happens to most lefties who are forced to adapt in a world of right-handers. I also prefer to have my more agile, trained hand on the fishing line.   A good cast always means your rod ends down, horizontal, level with the water. After casting, leave a loop of line in the hand that is not balancing the fly rod. With this hand, in my case the left hand, you can keep better control of the fishing line. (You need to prevent drag. Drag means your line has twisted in the stream or has wrapped about in a current or pool in such a way as to preceed your fly, which might make your fly look unnatural to the fish.) You fly fish with both your rod hand and your line hand.

Good casting takes practice, but casting well can be satisfying in itself and helps compensate for long intervals of no fish, helping a fisher develop patience. Practicing casting technique in the water is best, but you can practice in the park or back yard also. If you have a wheelbarrow or old tire, you can practice casting into that, filled with water, if you like. A good cast has particular feel to it. A good cast is a beautiful cast, and it's beautiful because it feels so. Such a cast feels effortless, and the line seems to take on a life of its own, sweeping through the air, arriving silently on the water, the fly dropping so lightly that the water is hardly dimpled. Over time, when you become comfortable and confident with your casts, and stop anguishing over their quality, you will find that you simply begin to cast naturally, almost absently. So who do we cast the spell on, ourselves or the fish?

'imitive Fishing

Fisherman
The wind blows the line out from his fishing rod.
In a straw hat and grass cape the fisherman
Is invisible in the long reeds.
In the fine spring rain it is impossible to see very far
And the mist rising from the water has hidden the hills.

Ou Yang Hsiu, 1007-1072, translated by Kenneth Rexroth

Nothing puts you on the cusp of experience, inside the moment, or outside of time, like catching a fish with a light fly rod. The lighter the rod, the more electric the fish feels, the nearer you are to no-rod, to no-fishing. I have heard tell of water currents electrifying the fishing line, and since most rods these days are graphite, charging the rod as if it were for divining not water, but those alive within it. Though I am sure fly fishers have been struck by lightning, I have never heard of anyone dying from electrical shock caused by stream currents. Possibly at ninety I will welcome such a death.

Paradoxically, fly fishing is a primitive form of angling; its rustic quality is what makes its beauty. People lose sight of the fact that fly fishing is primitive perhaps because there is more skill involved than other types of fishing, and many foolishly assume that greater skill and knowledge equate with technical advancement. But all the technological changes in fly fishing, lighter and stronger leaders and lines, graphite rods, more durable reels, all serve to enhance the primitive simplicity of fly fishing. Because of all the glitz and mystique surrounding fly fishing, perhaps a certain elitism born of the expensiveness of top of the line, new equipment, and perhaps the arcana of fly fishing has obscured its primitive essence. New rods, reels, jackets, and all the other paraphernalia can get expensive, but fly angling is not a fishing style for only the rich. The new stuff is great, but you can find superb used equipment, which hunting for can be fun.

Second-hand fly rods are abundant in antique stores and small tackle shops near well known trout streams.. Frequently, used fly rods are like brand-new because they were hardly ever used. Maybe their owners simply got frustrated with the art of fly fishing, or never had enough free time to practice. Maybe they had intentions to live out their lives fishing, but life, or death, got in their way. An older, well made fly rod, if seldom used, or used properly, or at least not abused, remains like new for many decades. A fly rod is an artfully crafted instrument, and an old one, well made, never loses its talismanic power. Used reels can be found in the same places as fly rods, and you might pick up a fishing jacket at a yard sale. Other than fishing line, leaders and flies, everything else is optional. Many fly fishers make their own flies, and I have met some who have also hand crafted their own rods. If you are so inclined, you can order kits to make your own bamboo rods.

The Latin word from which primitive comes is *Primitivus*, meaning original, related to beginnings, first formed, strongly suggesting purest, or first. According to the Oxford English Dictionary the implication is the same. The example given: *"Primitive Church,"* the Christian Church in its earliest and, by implication, purest times. For the last several centuries in the Western world, primitive lost its root meaning, and came to signify backwards, or inferior. It seems, strangely enough, that the early meaning of the word appears to be returning. A combination of factors has caused this, including the recognition of primitivism as a form of artistic expression, and a growing regard for the visionary aspects of those cultures that are, or were, uncluttered with linear reasoning and technological devices. Primitive anything is harder. Bow hunting and musket hunting are harder than using a high-powered rifle. Baking a cake from scratch is harder than using a mix. Fly fishing is harder than any other kind of fishing. Time after time other fishermen in passing have looked admiringly at my fly rod and remarked, "I tried to learn that but just didn't have the patience for it."

Patience, I am sure, is an expression of faith, but how one develops patience is hard to say. Stubbornness? A refusal to give up? Why do we think of so-called primitive people who lived by primitive techniques as having more patience than moderns? Were their options simply fewer, or is there something about life they may have understood better than we do? What is the key to developing patience so that one may join the rest of us madmen and madwomen in our devotion to fly fishing as the best way to fish, or the best way to live? There is no key. Yet I do believe that the best way to fish seems to involve balancing one's desire to catch fish with not caring too much. I am convinced that trout sense the energy of desire running through a fisherman's hands and arms, down through the fishing line like voltage that keeps the fish away.

29

Several factors make fly fishing primitive, including the lightness of the rod. The lighter the rod the more one feels the fish. Some purists fish with only bamboo fly rods, but the feel is just as good with older fiberglass rods and the contemporary graphite rods. I have used all three and can attest to no difference in the experience. I have no problem with the purist, but the lightweight graphite rods are my preference. Next is the fly reel, which has no spinner mechanism, so is old-fashioned in a way, and the fisher holds a loop of the line in hand to prepare for another cast or to feel a fish bite. When a fish is on you feel the fish with both the hand holding the rod and the hand with the fishing line. There is less separating you from the moment. Using fly patterns that imitate real creatures has to be an ancient practice going well back in time before recorded history. It is noteworthy that the Japanese, before they picked up on Western style fly fishing, practiced a form of fly fishing called Tenkara, translated as *from heaven*. The traditional rod, developed in the Japanese Alps and made specifically for small stream fishing, is constructed from bamboo, and can be retracted to two feet long or stretched dramatically up to thirteen feet, with a ten foot line and no reel. Apparently Japanese fishers made a living using this primitive form of fly fishing for centuries until after World War II, when modern "improvements" like damming made this form of commercial fishing impossible.

Perhaps Tenkara will catch on in the United States, but there are several factors that might prevent it from becoming the latest craze. One is that Tenkara is suitable for catching small fish, not trophies. Americans like big. Second is that this technique apparently works best on wild fish in small, remote streams. Personally I love finding small, wild fish in remote streams, but such streams can be hard to get to, not necessarily because they are in isolated regions of the Blue Ridge Mountains or the Rockies, but because such streams are just hard to negotiate. You may have to hike to reach such a stream, part of the beauty of it all, you may have to scrabble your way through difficult brush, and once you reach the water, you have to do a balancing act in a rocky creek. Streams like this are practically everywhere in the U.S. and Canada. If you are not a city dweller, there are probably several right around the corner from where you live. The third reason I think Tenkara might not catch on here is that it's just too simple. Fishing without a reel may be too naked for most westerners.

So, you have your rod, reel, and fishing line, the line being lightweight so that it floats on the water, and florescent yellow, orange, or green so you can see where your cast has gone. Attached to the fishing line is a leader line, and attached to that is tippet line, thin and wispy to go undetected by the trout, and the fly is knotted to the end of the tippet. All this stuff is well-crafted and for that reason can be expensive, the craftedness being part of the art's primitivism, paradoxically harder to make than mass produced tackle used for other types of fishing. We like to think people made good stuff in the old days, and they did if they took pride in their craft and wanted their creations to last. I have mentioned that excellent fly rods and reels can be gotten second hand. One can learn to make flies, but new ones aren't all that costly, and one doesn't need designer jackets and waders to fly fish, unless how you look while fishing is important to you.

What is really needed is to fall into the rhythm of your casts. The water can mesmerize you, the spray and the birds and sunlight cast their spells on you. Let them. At times you will forget that you are fishing.

Locating Fish in Small Streams

When I slip quietly (or blunder, trying to slip quietly) into a small stream, not only will I not encounter tubes or boats, but I'll be the only fisher in the water. Most fly anglers, like other fishers, wade into bigger waters for bigger fish, and cast long, the idea being that a cast from afar is less likely to reveal the angler's presence. I take my light fly rod, and go dry flying, making shorter more precise casts, or just letting the leader line wander down stream, naturally. In White Creek the banks are above my head, so that the landscape beyond isn't visible.

The banks are redolent with honeysuckle, thick with red twig dogwood, and the ubiquitous chipping of Red-winged black birds. There are also yellow warblers and orioles. Beyond the banks are phlox, purple and white, and beyond them cornfields. I am hidden in the stream, but through openings in the bank I can see silos in the distance. Where are the fish? Along the banks are willow trees, many of the willows leaning into the water. There are also deep pools, where the fish are on the warmer days.

The fish also hide under the banks, but when active they are in the pools and slower currents along the banks, or in the pools where there is submerged grass, or before and behind tufts of grass waving in the stream. Or before and behind a larger rock, which opens a small band of slower water for the trout to rest and to feed. When I began fly fishing I expected fish to always lie behind rocks, especially big rocks, but often they are in front because currents are slowed there, food is found more easily in front than behind a rock, and the pressure in front of rocks can make slight depressions for trout to rest. Often where there are currents in the stream, there are pools and eddies along the banks. Inside these pools are fish. In the currents near the pools, along the edges between pool and eddy, slower current and faster current, in the deeper water, are the fish. In small streams, expect trout in the deeper water.

One helpful method for finding fish in small streams is to search for the thalweg, a word of German origin meaning the lowest part of a valley, in this case an underwater valley. Thalwegs occur in pools, and are simply the deepest part of the channel that runs through a pool. Often the fastest current runs through the thalweg, so the most fish food is carried there. Hence, the greater likelihood of trout presence. So how does one find thalwegs? First, look for pools. But finding pools and depressions is not enough. One must also pay attention to currents and how they are moving in and around pools. I have also often made the mistake of fishing in pools that are deep and turbulent, believing they are ideal for trout. Too much turbulence, too much current, can be too powerful for trout, which seem to prefer gentle currents and mild turbulence. Anyone who has any familiarity with trout knows how fussy they are. Things must be Just Right. If not, trout will move to where conditions are closest to Just Right.

As the season progresses, the deeper water becomes less frequent, but more important to the fish, and these places are easier to find fish, but it's much more fun to find them in the spring, when deeper water along the creek is most everywhere, and you feel blessed to see a fish rise, or have to go on instinct and luck, on faith that there are trout in that spinning pool in front of those submerged willow boughs that span the stream. I like both. I like seeing a fish rise, so that I know I'm fishing where there is at least one fish. But I also like going on faith. Or instinct, or skill, or luck. Call it what you will. When you've seen a fish rise that's luck, too. A gift. We must take our gifts where they find us.

The more you're in the water, somehow, the more you begin to sense where the trout are. I am trying my best to explain this, and even verbalizing the techniques of finding trout in small streams feels awkward. In time you get an instinct for it all. The trout just aren't going to be in the middle of the stream unless it's deeper or as deep as the water along the bank. They are most always in or near pools in the water made by springs under the stream, spring pools. The trout are usually going to be where there's cover, trees or bushes overhanging the water. And in such places, if you're not careful, you can snag your fly in the branches and leaves in the stream. So use care. Don't let your line run very far. Judge just how far it can go without getting caught. You don't need to get precisely under that fallen willow or maple. That's seldom possible. Fish before the deadfall, around and after it, where there are eddies and twisting current that will make your fly waver naturally.

Another factor involved in finding fish is the fact that there may be long stretches in streams where there are no fish. Over time the value of exploring local streams will pay off so that, eventually, you will always know where to locate fish and will not waste valuable angling time. When you fish in a small stream or brook, you may be the only person who will fish there that year. Maybe the only person who has fished there in years. The sky is softer blue than usual, the stratus clouds majestic as always. The sunlight spangling the water almost tricks you sometimes, but you know whether or not that was a trout rising. When you are fishing in a small trout stream, in that time, in that moment, you are the only one fishing there, ever.

The Numen

What of this fondness for fishing in small streams and creeks? Though they can be hard to find and difficult to navigate, there is something special about fishing in your own secret place where nobody ever goes. The trout in these streams are usually small, and always wild, unschooled in the ways of that odd genus of human, the fly fisher. The fish can be found in or near small, crystalline, swirling pools, deep enough to hide them, where a tree has fallen, across the stream, or, even better, at an odd angle, leaving a current or riffle along the edge of the bank. They often hide in cutbanks under tree roots, where the bank overhangs the stream. You have to be careful approaching these spots, because if the fish see you they'll get frantic and dive, or race back and forth across the pool, too spooked to bite. You do not want to "amaze" the trout, as Izaak Walton described. You also have to take care not to let your shadow fall into the pool. Trout, skittish by nature, seem to have an uncanny, innate ability to distinguish a cloud or bird's shadow from a human's, particularly a human with a fly rod in hand. The beauty of these creeks and brooks where so few people visit is that you can sense a presence in them, perhaps akin to Shinto, or what native Americans have often expressed about particular places.

Perhaps one of the reasons some Amerindian cultures left so few traces of their past was because they had no sense of linear time in the way we do. Their mythos was often a present manifestation. Maybe there existed a sense, like the aboriginal people of Australia, that nature is an artist whose visual works needed no embellishments or alterations. Why make wooden or stone sculptures of spirit shapes when those spirits are ever-present in trees and in rocks, their voices the wind and running water? Perhaps that is why so many sites, redolent of spirit, were left naked and pristine, without a trace of human imprint. One might think of Tibetan mandalas, made of sand, metaphorical of infinity, created to be erased. Some human imprints are made to soon vanish into the landscape.

Catch and Release

Without death, there can be no beauty. Zen fishers also know the relationship between beauty and death, either consciously or non-verbally down in their bones, and in their blood. That's the joy of playing a trout, or landing one. That's why they practice catch and release. Not simply because they may be among the hopelessly romantic, which some fly fishers probably are, but because they are making the mad attempt to position themselves outside the circle of death and birth, so that they may witness its power. Often that which contains beauty may not feel its own beauty. So to stand, or wade, outside of beauty becomes a back door way of entering into it. But why fish for trout? Beyond their fierce resistance to capture, I believe we fish for trout because of their beauty. The brown trout, with its black spots against a green and golden backdrop, the iridescent green and rainbow wash of the rainbow trout, the red spots and blue halos and deep green of the brook trout, all in living form, resonate with something deeply encoded in us. Much has been speculated about humanity's destructive hereditary qualities, but an aesthetic sense, a need for beauty, is also in our nature. The places where wild fish thrive are places we need, not simply for our physical survival, but for all those intangibles that make life glimmer.

When releasing a trout, if the hook is attached to the fish's gills or stomach, simply cut the fly line with your snips. You'll do more damage trying to free the trout, and the hook will eventually rust away. Keep your hands wet when releasing the fish, and don't wipe off its oily coating. Try to get your fish quickly back into the water. It's tempting to continue admiring, but it's not good for fish to be too long out of the water. Fish, like humans, can die of shock and can be only briefly out of their element.

The Trout Mafia

Never call your fly rod a fishing pole. If word gets out, the Trout Mafia, a renegade, pariah band reputed by unreliable sources to consist of disgruntled Trout Unlimited members, will come after you. Your fly rod is your samurai sword, magic wand, divining tool, which links you to sacred water, to fish, and, hopefully, the divine. A fishing pole is a more homely device used by guys with names like Huck Finn and Uncle Bob. People who fish with fly rods have names like Ted Williams, Izaak Walton, Amelia Earhart, and Ernest Hemingway.

A Hover of Trout, a Lie of Trout

In *An Exaltation of Larks* James Lipton explores the venereal game, a medieval form of phrase-making in English that often includes punning. For example, a murder of crows, a parliament of owls, a host of angels, a pride of lions. These terms of venery become collective nouns. Young gentlemen were taught them from Books of Venery, in part so that they might learn correct designations for their quarry. The more clever student could invent his own. Lipton points out that school of fish is a corruption, perhaps through repeated error, of shoal of fish, a shoal being a stretch of shallow water. Lipton's book provides one example for trout, a hover of trout, and trout do indeed hover in water. Here are my entries:

A tremble of trout, a trickle of trout, a college of trout, a transit of trout, a cast of trout, a leap of trout, a flight of trout, a bed of trout, a streak of trout, a gaggle of trout, a bale of trout, a stream of trout, a crew of trout, a collage of trout, a cloud of trout, a brook of trout, a tangle of trout, a coven of trout, a cloister of trout, a trance of trout, a hive of trout, a cauldron of trout, a trickery of trout, a cast of flies, a committee of trout, a constellation of trout, a bend of trout, a babble of trout, a recital of trout, a meander of trout, a tentativeness of trout, a timidity of trout, a coolness of trout, a bevy of trout, an audience of trout, a tumble of trout, a tremor of trout, a travail of trout, a dalliance of trout, a tribe of trout. A lie of trout, a speckling of trout, a chimera of trout, an intrepidness of trout, a percolation of trout, a tenacity of trout, a perseverance of trout, a tickle of trout, a feistiness of trout, a tingle of trout, a faintness of trout, a file of fingerlings, a fry of trout, a perspicacity of trout, a spawn of trout, a fain of trout, a tabernacle of trout, a fickleness of trout, a pool of rainbows, a brood of browns, a Bravery of browns, a breach of brookies, a fable of fly fishers. A lie of trout.

Witch Fly

Which fly to choose? Picking the "right" fly or pattern, that tiny
dummy fly the fish will perceive as real, often makes all the difference.
The right fly will catch you a fish. The wrong one will not. In many
situations several patterns will work. Other times only one will lure the
fish. What I have learned is that there are at least several patterns that
are consistently effective in most fly fishing environments here in the
northeast. The nymph flies I like best are Pheasant Tails and various
varieties of Bead Head Nymphs, gold or silver, particularly the
silver-headed Lightning Bugs, and the Prince Nymphs, especially The
Fly Formerly Known As Prince. The Flashback Hare's Ear is also
effective.

How to find out which flies work best: experimentation (trying out
different patterns), scientific method, trial and error, reading books and
articles on fly fishing, asking the fish themselves, practice, dreams,
intuition. On several occasions fly fishers themselves have described
their successes. Once a tall, gaunt fisher whose age was hard for me to
gauge, though I suspect, belying his fitness and intensity, that he was in
his early eighties, told me about catching 15 browns in a stretch of the
Battenkill not far from a bridge. I consider catching 15 trout in a
morning, an evening, or even a day something of an accomplishment, a
halcyon day for a fly fisher. He had my full attention.

Having fished unsuccessfully in the spot for some time (fly fishers are
notoriously vague about time because we lose our habitual sense of it
while angling), a caddis fly landed on his hand. Now such an
occurrence might be read as an omen, but omens are useless unless one
can read them. We might also call it good naturalist's fishing logic. In
short, he had the good sense to take a caddis pattern out of the little fly
box a good fly fisher keeps in his fishing jacket. Thus it was with a
caddis fly pattern he caught his fifteen. Of course what the veteran
angler did was use common sense, but when one considers all those
elements that get in the way of observation, perhaps common sense, as
others have noted, is not so common.

The lesson is that paying close attention to what's around is
indispensable. Sometimes I try to observe what's falling into the
stream, to watch the insects swarming above the surface, or choose the
fly that's been biting me. I have derived grand sadistic pleasure from

slapping a deer fly, and flicking his stunned, still living body into the water and then witnessing a fish instantly snapping him up, and out of this world. Often, however, it's difficult to identify just exactly what it is the fish are rising for. The ephemerals may be too tiny to make out. There are many informative works that identify, with pictures or photographs, just what time of the season certain trout delicacies are hatching. The Blue-winged Olive, for example, hatches during various times of the spring, summer, and fall in the northeast. Therefore the Olive is a popular choice when one is in doubt. One can make a study of different crustaceans, flies, and ephemerals and the times of the season they emerge, taking into account weather and climate variations. Despite myself, I have learned some of this not so esoteric esoterica. What's great about fly fishing, though, is that it is an art, not an exact science. I like better to test my luck, and intuition, advanced instinct in human beings.

An addendum to the ancient fisher's story is that the following year he returned to the same spot where he caught the remarkable 15. He ruefully explained that he had no luck; there wasn't a fish there. I think he was rueful because he feared the fish had disappeared because something was wrong. The trout's habitat had deteriorated, or they were over-fished by someone not catch-and-releasing, or they had vanished because of some other environmental decline that all good fly fishers dread. A site where you've made memorable catches becomes akin to sacred, and to return and find no fish there feels like a loss of grace, or providence, providence as divine luck.

But I have another take on the fisher's experience. He had entered the zone, as athletes call it, or had an artistic inspiration. He was in the right place at the right time in the right state of mind and all his being and his senses were cued to the fish, the water, the weather, even the stars hidden in the sky. He had entered a space out-of-time, in synchronicity with an otherness. Such experiences are, as he knew, quite rare, and impossible to duplicate. And rightfully so. What's duplicatable is perhaps not worth attempting. I am sure he knew all this, and was not really after duplication. One or two fish caught would have pleased him. Possibly the fish had simply moved on, up river or down river. Perhaps they had slipped through time. Yet he still rued that there were no fish there like a lover who had been stood up, more worried that his partner had been harmed than covetous for her embrace. Because I am a proverbial hopeless romantic, I loved the old, noble fisher for his hurt.

Neglect and Fly Fever

It may happen that you catch what is known informally by those who have it as Fly Fever, or Fish Fever. You most likely catch the disease after fly fishing for awhile. For several years of fly fishing I was somewhat psychologically healthy, free of obsession, then one year I caught Fly Fever and am forever in its throes, which I don't mind – a symptom of the disease itself. Fortunately in my case I was, and still am, living near the Battenkill when I came down with St. Peter's Passion in its most virulent form, so its effects didn't disrupt my life too badly, but I dread to think what would have happened if there weren't a trout stream nearby to slake my need to fish. When you catch this fever people who do not fly fish will not understand your obsession, and think you are perhaps a bit mad, if not outright insane. But because you are only fishing, there isn't much anyone will do about it except complain about being neglected. What I'm calling fever or madness, isn't really, but the fisher possessed of an enlightened state. I have found it better, though, to describe this enlightened state (and you do indeed feel lighter) as a fever in order to keep people at bay. Fever they understand. Enlightenment, who knows?

Neglect is problematic in two ways: livelihood and relationships. If you are ignoring your livelihood because of the fever, you may sell your house and car and whatever else you have that you really don't need so that you can buy a smaller place nearer the trout stream you like. You realize that you will need to get by on less if you're going to be fishing more than working. Perhaps what is required is a type of passive tenacity, one that artists have who risk everything, especially financial security, for their avocation. As in the manner French artists greet and leave one another, *Courage.*

Relationships could be jeopardized by the fever. If you have children hopefully they'll have grown before the fever takes you away. If you have teenagers they'll be glad you're out of their hair. If you have a partner or mate, hopefully they're the understanding type. They might take up the practice also, though I think of fly angling as a solitary practice. I am sure there are trout widowers, though I haven't met one yet. As for trout widows, I am not sure how to console them, but to

41

suggest they take up the fishing themselves. This is an individual and personal matter. There really aren't many good excuses for neglecting loved ones, which presents a real problem for us fevered ones. Just tell them that closeness is a state of mind. Good luck. And *courage*.

Roll Cast

One can make an argument that being self-taught to fly fish is better than being formally instructed, and vice versa. I'm not sure I'd recommend being self-taught over formally taught, though in my case I would not like to change. I might have saved lots of time and frustration had I learned to fish from instruction. I learned through reading, picking the brains of older fly anglers and, most of all, through trial and error. One thing is for certain, learning through experience is irreplaceable. What an angler knows through experience is solid, especially when that fisher hears things that contest his own experience. One can make big generalizations about fishing, but particular experiences in particular streams sometimes defy conventional wisdom and although fish species have generalized behaviors, fish sometimes behave with individual quirkiness. Just ask any angler who has spent a lot of time fishing for rainbows.

My experience with the roll cast might put the issue in an interesting perspective. Learning to cast is not all that difficult, especially if someone shows you, and the key is to cast lightly, maintaining a two o'clock—ten o'clock arc. But no one ever showed me how to roll cast, and when I tried to find instruction in books I found the whole thing baffling. The irony is that when I was looking up roll casting I already knew how to do it, and quite well, as a matter of fact. I simply did not realize what I was doing was called roll casting, which is casting with a short amount of leader and line in tight situations. When there is no way to back cast because of brush and trees, you simply take a short amount of line, sometimes only leader line, and flip the line into the water flicking your wrist. I developed this technique on my own (a little bit like reinventing the waffle iron) because in tight, small stream settings, there was no other way to get my fly into the water where I knew there were fish.

One of the many virtues of fishing alone is no one sees you screwing up. I cannot begin to calculate how many bushes and trees I caught in tight stream situations. It was either stop fishing in these wild places, or learn to improvise—in my case, the improvisation was roll casting. And, strangely enough, I was feeling inadequate about not knowing something that I already knew quite well. If there is a drawback to being self-taught, I believe it's often these little gaps that in most cases don't matter much, and can be rather funny.

Snips and Zingers

Snips are indispensable. You will always need them to trim the excess tippet line you'll have after knotting your fly to your leader line with a cinch knot. Untrimmed tippet line will make your fly look freakish to fish, as though your nymph has grown a wild antenna or developed a butterfly's proboscis. Such a sight will cause a trout either to gape at the fly incredulously, or to flee in terror. Of all the doodads involved in fly fishing, snips are a necessity and easy to lose, but a nail clipper will work almost as well.

There is another doohickey called a zinger, a metal, compass-like apparatus that pins onto your fly jacket. The first time I saw a zinger in a tackle store and asked the guy what it was, he looked at me like I had read him a line of poetry in Romanian, then off-handedly explained that the zinger's only purpose is to make it easier to use your snips. Snips clip onto the zinger which together looks like a naval medallion for bravery, and the zinger has a little cord that functions like tape measure. You simply pull the snips when you need them, and they return via the zinger's automatic retractable cord when you are done. Otherwise losing snips can get expensive. You may need to use snips in many situations, like cutting your fly line caught on something, or even to free a fish badly hooked, or to save yourself when a giant brown begins pulling you into deep water.

The Five Golden (or Speckled) Skills of Fly Angling

There are no five golden elements or skills of fly angling. If there were, they would be these, and in this order: One, finding fish; Two, fly selection; Three, stealth; Four, casting; Five, luck.

Finding Fish: I believe you can enjoy fly fishing without catching anything, but it's all the better if you land trout, or at least have many good fights with them. If you cannot find where they are, you'll seldom catch them, even if you are good at everything else. Finding fish requires reading the water, and this requires practiced imagining, observation, and exploration.

Fly Selection: If you are using a lure or pattern the trout aren't interested in, you're simply not going to convince them to bite, no matter how stubborn or wishful you are. Experiment with different flies, paying close attention to what's flying around you and what's flittering around the banks and the stream's surface.

Stealth: Fish can hear, fish can see. Move quietly as possible through the water. Avoid wearing your old disco suit. If you are wearing swimming trunks, don't wear those fancy floral ones from Bermuda, the Cook Islands, or Old Navy. Plainer colors that blend like tans, browns, greens are best. The color blue is okay too. Again, use imagination and common sense. The shallower the water, the more easily fish can see you. Cast from a location or angle where you simply cannot be visible to the fish unless they poke their heads above the surface. The only times trout do this is when they rise for some insect, and when they do so they are so intent on that creature they do not notice your presence. Remain still once you find a spot you can realistically cast from without their sighting you. Do not underestimate the trout's ability to sense danger. Often trout seem downright psychic.

Casting: Sloppy casting is more likely to catch you than to catch a fish. Frustration is the arch-enemy of all fly anglers, and getting yourself tangled in your own line, especially if other people are around, is profoundly discouraging. It's also annoying to get your fly caught in the saplings and brush along the banks and overhead. Even with this knowledge, and with the smallest of fly rods, I still manage more than occasionally to catch my fly on a branch or bush. That's simply a hazard of fishing, particularly in small streams. Don't try to be too

45

fancy with your casting. Better to make a shorter, say fifteen foot, cast that's smooth, light, and accurate, than to frustrate yourself constantly trying to make that so-called classic 30 foot cast. Start out with shorter casts. Focus on accuracy and lightness. In fly angling, the most artistic element is the cast, which should be graceful, the line dropping into the water before the delicate fly falls in. Accuracy and softness are more important than distance. Don't feel discouraged by those showoffs who can cast 100 feet. Such feats of prowess have little or nothing to do with catching fish, aren't necessary for catching fish in big rivers, and are ridiculously impossible in small streams. Often you simply need to roll cast in small streams; make a short cast by flicking the rod with your wrist. Distance of casting improves over time, as does accuracy, but given the choice, I prefer accuracy. If you can cast accurately 20 to 25 feet, that's easily enough for small streams.

Luck: Baseball pundit Branch Rickey once said, "Luck is the residue of design." The previous four elements are of design. I have no formulae for luck, or providence. There is only patience, and the focused love of being a useless fisher in a trout stream. Patience, of course, is the sixth skill of fly fishing.

How to Recognize a Zen Fly Fishing Master

I have read that many Buddhists believe in the existence of extraterrestrial life forms, including intelligent alien species, and that they do not feel spiritually threatened in any way by the possibility, if not the probability of beings from outer space. Somehow calling aliens "beings" seems Zen-like in itself. However, my understanding is that most Buddhist monks respond to the question about the existence of intelligent aliens with, *Yes, they exist. So?* So, how do you recognize a fly fishing master? *Why on earth would you want to?* William Butler Yeats has a poem about that sometimes ghostly, elusive, often solitary being he called "The Fisherman":

Although I can see him still,
The freckled man who goes
To a grey place on a hill
In grey Connemara clothes
At dawn to cast his flies,
It's long since I began
To call up to the eyes
This wise and simple man.
All day I looked in the face

What I had   hoped 'twould be
To write for my own race
And the reality;
The living men that I hate,
The dead man that I loved,
The craven man in his seat,
The insolent unreproved,
And no knave brought to book
Who has won a drunken cheer,
The witty man and his joke
Aimed at the commonest ear,
The clever man who cries
The catch-cries of the clown,
The beating down of the wise
And great Art beaten down.

Maybe a twelvemonth since
Suddenly I began,
In scorn of this audience,
Imagining a man,
And his sun-freckled face,
And grey Connemara cloth,
Climbing up to a place
Where stone is dark under froth,
And the down-turn of his wrist
When the flies drop in the stream;
A man who does not exist,
A man who is but a dream;
And cried, "Before I am old
I shall have written him one
Poem maybe as cold
And passionate as the dawn."

Woolly Buggers

Fishermen study fish, not in search of truth for its own sake as does the biologist, because truth in this instance represents the exotic.

Harold Blaisdell

Many fly fishers would agree that if there were only one artificial lure available to them for the remainder of their lives, that lure would be the Woolly Bugger. Such anglers would not be purists in the sense that the Woolly Bugger is not a dry fly, a lure fished on the stream's surface, and it in no way matches the hatch. The Woolly Bugger is a streamer, a class of lures that resemble bait creatures like minnows, though in fact the Bugger, as its name implies, doesn't seem to imitate anything in nature. The Woolly Bugger is an exotic, provocative lure, essentially a monstrosity. Buggers are usually large as fly angling patterns go, a couple of inches in length, and come in all sorts of colors, purple, white, black, orange, brown, russet, green, whatever. They sometimes look similar to dragonflies in that they've goggle eyes fused to a bulging head, but their bodies taper into predominantly long wisps of hair and, if not solid colored, iridescent feathers, sparkling green, gold, or red.

Some say that Woolly Buggers resemble leeches, but that's a real stretch. I've pulled leeches off after fishing in Black Creek, brought them home in a jar of clear water, and watched them up close. Once the leeches unfold, you can see they are highly aggressive, strong swimmers, but they look nothing like Woolly Buggers which, once cast, have a graceful, dream-like motion as they disappear into the stream. No, Woolly Buggers, like the Grey Ghost or the Shushan Postmaster, like most streamers, are provocative lures that don't closely imitate anything known on planet earth. So why at certain times, do so many species of fish, including trout, salmon, and small mouth bass, go ape-shit over them? Why do they attack them with such reckless abandon, especially trout, which are habitually so suspicious, so finicky that they often reject nearly perfect imitations? There are no perfect imitations.

"There are more things in heaven and earth, Horatio, Than are dreamt of in your philosophy," claims Hamlet. One is the Woolly Bugger, and perhaps all exotic lures. There are many riddles in this world that we will never answer. Many of these mysteries we do not need to solve, but there is nothing wrong with wondering. Maybe obsessive searches might lead to experiences that are powerful in and of themselves. I like to take many things on faith, like why some fish will attack a Woolly Bugger.

I do have my own theory, however, which can never be proven by scientific method, or even informal experimentation. What I believe is that the Woolly Bugger, when trawled herky-jerky through the water, or cast so that it moves freely through a stream's current, is an abomination, a monstrosity to a salmon, a trout, a small mouth. The bugger somehow triggers a wild aggression in the fish. Though the bugger is an anomaly, a horror, it's a non-threatening one, perhaps because of its size, otherwise the fish would flee, rather than pursue. Somehow, deeply coded in the fish's genetic structure, reaching back through eons, there is something in the fish that is provoked, some mechanism is triggered by the appearance of the Bugger, even though the fish has never encountered such a creation, nor has any of its relatives over millions of years of evolution. You could actually look at the Woolly Bugger, and all other unnatural and exotic lures that trout chase, as just more evidence of evolutionary behavior. As nothing like the Bugger or The Fly Formerly Known as Prince occurs in nature, could it be that there exists some flexibility in fish behavior that allows for adaptation, which, in turn, enhances their chances for survival? We know that evolution, though slow, is a dynamic process. If, through eons of evolution, something resembling a Woolly Bugger were to appear, we can feel confident that some species of fish are already prepared for this new being under the sun, or water, as it were.

Perhaps the Bugger is a sort of tiny Frankenstein that the fish *feels* it can easily eliminate from its perfect existence. Maybe the Bugger simply looks good to eat. Perhaps the fish is witnessing the most delectable form of living food (all wild fish food is eaten alive) that has crossed its field of vision. One can speculate but never really know. I, for one, do not need to know; I am thankful for the madman who invented the Woolly Bugger. His invention, a work of imagination and genius; his first fish caught with the weird charm, is an act of great discovery in the big little world of fly angling. Perspective is always important, so I like to keep in mind that the discovery of the effectiveness of the Woolly Bugger pattern is meaningful only to fly anglers, and thus of Lilliputian grandeur. Why certain fish at certain times go crazy for this lure will remain forever a mystery, and empirical theories will always have something lacking. Are there things we might be attracted to, or repelled by, even though we have never seen or imagined them before?

50

Fish Where You Are

Perhaps it is too easy advice for me to give, that fishing nearby is the best way to fly fish. If you do not live near a trout stream, then you should move. For many who are not urbanites, somewhere nearby there are ponds, streams, lakes, or the ocean. Even anglers in New York City are cognizant that they are living on an island with the ocean close by. You don't need a trout stream to fly fish, and all kinds of fish are fun to catch. I cannot tell you how often I have traveled for hours to try fishing in some new and far off place, only to find that the fishing was better closer to home.

Small cities, towns, villages, often have small streams nearby. Why fish them? They have wild trout in them, for one thing. For another, probably no one fishes them. And, finally, they can be easily reached. How much actual angling time is lost by fishers driving long distance to places far from work or home isn't something that needs to be calculated to determine that the answer is *too much time*. I suspect that people fail to go fishing after a day's work, for example, because the desired river is too distant, the destination requiring too much additional labor. Locating a good little stream close to home makes for many more hours of quality goof-off time.

The question is, then, why are so many good little trout streams near home usually ignored? For one thing, most brooks and creeks are small, providing habitat only for small fish. But a wild, six to nine inch brook trout is a joy to catch on a light-weight rod. Angling with a one-or two-weight line is ideal for small streams. I cannot stress this enough. Light-weight rods and reels are key to enjoying small stream fishing. Most spinner reel fishers angle in ponds, lakes, rivers where they can catch large fish. Short rods are suitable for tight, short, precise casts. Many people probably think the brook under the bridge by the hometown post office is too small to sustain fish, or is polluted. Are anglers, like most of us, creatures of habit and imitation? We do not fish in the creek behind the abandoned factory because no one else does; it has never dawned on us to do so. Perhaps we tend to feel that the exotic experience, or just the fun experience, can never be in our back yard, but must be at least an hour's drive away. How often does an angler consider that a good fishing hole is within walking distance?

Spirit Fish

In the night I dreamed of trout-fishing; and, when at length I awoke, it seemed a fable that this painted fish swam there so near my couch, and rose to our hooks the last evening, and I doubted if I had not dreamed it all.

From *Ktaadn Trout*, Henry David Thoreau

Trout exist outside of time, except when a fly fisher plays and lands one; then the fisherman's time and the trout's no-time converge in an extended moment. Facing upstream effortlessly in gentle currents, trout live in glorious stasis. Fish are emblematic of the life force with their streamlined bodies born of water. They are denizens of a liquid world so like the interior universe that no cartographer can chart, but that we all visit, at least when we are dreaming, or imagining, drifting into those nether places, as naturally as the fish that dwell hidden under water. When we catch a trout, even when certain they are in a particular pool or stretch of current, there is always a sense of surprise, of spontaneity. When we release a trout, the fish evaporates back into the stream as though she were without substance, vanishing the way a dream does when we wake.

Quit Your Job

Where there is no creative originality, there is no Zen.

D. T. Suzuki

A good fly fisher learns something new every time astream. Such learning may not be measured quantitatively, but is certainly felt instinctively, taking you beyond mere knowledge into something more closely akin to wisdom. Most learning takes place inside the water and, as any good trout fisher knows, the best teachers are the trout themselves. Years and years of fly angling can lead to the accumulation of vast knowledge, but not necessarily. Professor George W. Harvey, the first to teach fly fishing at the university level, has said, "I know of many such anglers who have fished for years and believe they have had years of experience, when all they have is the first year's experience repeated over and over."

Harvey claims that the observations of many fly fishers are static, and therefore their years of experience are overrated. My argument is that you needn't have decades of experience in order to be a skillful fly angler, and the belief that you must have many years in the water has probably discouraged many people from abandoning the spinner reel and taking up the fly rod. The more open you are to experience, and flexible in your approaches to fishing, the more you can compress scores of years into mere seasons.

Nevertheless, the better you become at fly fishing, the more you will probably want to. And the best way to compress years of experience in a fishing season is to go fly angling for that entire season, which may create a crisis in one's personal life. I have little advice I can offer on this matter. If you have children, hopefully they are grown up and self-reliant, because if you are fishing all season and fly tying during the winter, you will be of little help to them. If you are married, or committed to a partner, perhaps they will join you in fishing or simply in meandering with you up and down trout streams, or, for whatever reason, not mind your long absences, or that far away look in your eyes, even when present. Hopefully they won't mind that you have stopped working, except perhaps in the winter, that you have moved near to your favorite trout stream, and that the only things you have left of any financial value are some fly rods and reels.

The Best Time to Fish

Zen fly fishers often give the same answer to this question:

"Any time you can."

Camouflage

I am ceaselessly amazed not only by the rich colors and patterns of trout, and fish in general, but also by how those patterns blend with the water. Lorian Hemingway, Ernest's granddaughter, describes her fight with her first blue marlin in "The Young Woman and the Sea":

"And I saw my friend standing on his tail in the water, moving that body that was all muscle and the same amount of fury. His color could never be duplicated, not even in the memory of Papa. He was shot with purple streaks, and his body threw off sparks of green and spinning marbles of sea water. He was as blue as the finest robe of the finest silk worn by the grandest Emperor of China. He stood in twisting power on the water as if he could walk, and threw his head furiously. His open mouth was that brilliant red seldom seen anywhere but in the most perfect of tropical flowers."

What stuns are the colors that emerge on the fish, be it a one pound brown trout or a 500 pound blue marlin. Not so much that these colors have evolved with the fish, or the fish have evolved with these colors, but that in the water such colors hide the fish. One would think their brilliance would do the opposite. The splendor of the fish is revealed only when brought into the suffocating air and flaming light. And the fish will do all it can to avoid being nakedly revealed, as if what it dreads most is being seen, not dying. A trout covets its naked beauty as fiercely as the goddess Diana. Fortunately, I have yet to hear of any fishermen changed into stags after capturing a trout. Perhaps no one has yet caught the fish who wields such power, or those who have have never been seen again.

The sleek, streamlined trout make one believe some alchemy of the stream has created the fish, its essence distilled, with all its dimpled colors of green and gold and red and pink and silver, compressed and embodied into a sentient being, fiercely alive, instinct-driven, wild, always the same temperature as the realm that delivered and still carries it. Perhaps the fish live in their element in the same way we are an embodiment, a compaction and distillation of something infinitely greater in scope than we are.

What seems miraculous is how a trout emerges from the water. How could something so marvelously painted remain so hidden? Yet blend they do. The patterns and colors on brooks, rainbows and browns are also quite different, yet all three disappear easily into water, water of differing depths, various floors of sand and rock, and always varying hues of blue, green, gold and white water. Sometimes I have spied a stream bed and noticed the colors of moss and marbled stones are precisely like the markings on a brown or brook trout. Sometimes, when I have lifted a rainbow out of the stream, it sparkles just like the water dancing beneath it. After releasing a trout, how simply it vanishes back whence it came, creating the illusion that it never existed in fish form before being caught, and is now re-absorbed by the river, as insubstantial as a daydream. To catch a trout is to be startled awake.

The First Commandment

Fly fishing instructors often speak of "Presentation," casting one's fly elegantly into the stream to tempt a trout. Presentation is sometimes called the first commandment of fly fishing. (Not true. The first commandment is to properly care for your fly rod. Keep it in its tube always except when you are preparing to use it. Care for it like a precious instrument, an appendage to the infinite.) The importance of Presentation, of delivering your fly lightly onto or into the stream, is fly fishing's most revealing characteristic as an art. I doubt if any two fly casts are exact. And I believe most fly fishers evolve their own style within the framework of what makes a good cast.

Therefore we have presentation, balance, patience, single-mindedness, many mindedness, no-mindedness, a breeze, rippling water, warbling birds, no mosquitoes (because of the breeze) occasional flies (for hints at what to fish with), and casts, casts uncoiling over the rushing stream. You are not trying to win a part in a play, to get a promotion, or to win a national championship or a Nobel Prize. You are not competing against nature or against yourself or against the trout. You feel good, but you are not relaxing. You are not doing penance, praying or meditating. You are simply fishing. Who and what you were or will become no longer matter. What you are is a fly fisher.

The Ones That Get Away

Because of the sheer fight in trout, the tiny aspect of fly hooks, and the fact that flies are lightly barbed or non-barbed, fish often get away. Escaping the hook happens more often with bigger fish because they are stronger. Is it not always big ones that are The Ones That Got Away? Therefore bringing them in requires, happily, a wilder, longer fight, but the longer the play, the longer the fish is still in his element, the more opportunities he has for escape. The fly fisher needs to let go after losing a fish, to be stoic, and to let disappointment vanish with the lost fish.

I once played a large brown not far from the railroad trestle bridge on the Battenkill. The bridge loomed overhead like a rust-colored ruin, and currents and riffles ran hard under it. Just before that bridge, the steep bank was thick with a mix of ancient white pines, oaks, sycamores, maples, and under them, in the fast current, a rock ledge, great habitat for trout. I had been casting perpendicular to the current, facing the stream, with the bridge to my right, when the trout hit. We had a long, zigzagging struggle. I got the fish just far enough out of the water to see his head, and to see him shake off the line and disappear back down under the rock ledge hidden by that fast-moving current. But I still felt good, and have played this same fish (I believe it is the same one) another time after. I have taken to calling him Big Daddy, though he could be a she. Male trout have more prominent, jutting jaws, but I've never gotten close enough to Big Daddy to see if he's really Big Momma.   Sometimes I think that for almost every fish I have caught, I have lost one. The reasons fly fishing is gratifying are the same as those that cause you to lose a fish. Sure, you could use triple barbed hooks with impaled worms squirming enticingly, and fish with heavy duty tackle. But you might as well fish with a super-sonar detector and a giant net. The delight of playing a fish, and of landing, is due to the lightness and miniature aspect of the fly tackle: the rod, reel, fishing line and fly. The trade-off is that a fly fisher is as likely to play and lose as often as play and win.

I am no longer nonplussed by the fact that losing fish is frequent, and that you can lose them at any time in the play, from shortly after they take the hook, to just as they rise out of the water as you reel them in. The latter occurrence could be reasonably regarded as a Catch if you are a catch-and-release fisher. After all, the fish has gotten herself off the hook, saving you the trouble, and detached herself quite cleanly and unharmed. At what point is a fish caught as opposed to lost? Or, as in *Moby Dick*, a fast fish or a loose fish? The fishing licenses say nothing about not lying, or exaggerating, and I think a fly fisher needs to give himself or herself as much credit and applause as possible. Therefore, a fish pulled completely out of the water can be termed a catch if your struggle with the fish warrants triumph.

There are important details to remind yourself. First, you were fishing in a place where there are fish, so your intuitive sonar is fine. Intuition, refined instinct in humans, is an important part of fly fishing, and even if fish were only hitting on your fly, to know that fish actually were where you were fishing has saved you from the absolute absurdity of fishing where no fish are. Second, your fly selection was good. A fish took your fly. Good. Of all the types of flies there are, the one you chose fooled the fish. Third, not only your pattern or fly, but the motion that you used was effective. After all, how bad could your casting be if fish were hitting on your fly? For some fly fishers, a good cast is as important as a catch. Fourth, your knots were right. If not, there would have been no play. The fish would have run off immediately with your fly. Fifth, you were able to play the fish, which is a thrilling fusion of fish, fisher, stream and moment. When the fish is lifted from the water, glittering, emerald wonder that he is, time begins again. Or it begins again once the fish is lost, or freed. After all, isn't fly angling for trout mostly about a way to see them?

Getting upset about losing a fish? You might as well get annoyed by the rain. I just remain in the water and check to see if the fly is still intact, then cast it back into the stream.

Zen

Zen is more akin to poetry than to logic or philosophy. I prefer standing in a stream to sitting (Zazen). To look for enlightenment may be the best way not to find it. Standing in a stream is better than sitting. Wading in a stream is better than pacing. Fishing is better than doing nothing, a better way of doing something that might appear as idleness to some. When you have a fish on, a trout bending your fly rod more slender than a birch branch, you do not think. You are cast inside a moment.

Desire

A strange phenomenon that occurs in all forms of fishing, perhaps even more so in fly fishing, is the capture of fish around the time when you are ready to quit. I have heard different explanations for success occurring at day or evening's end, but none has ever really satisfied me. My theory is that fish sense something different, or better, stop sensing something unnatural when the fisher is ready to quit. Fish, particularly wild fish, are highly sensitive, instinctive, and telepathic creatures. Although fish are similar in the sense that most species of fish look and behave like fish (just as all humans share similar characteristics), they can be individually different and quirky in the way humans can. I am not suggesting that they sense desire in the same way that we define the word, but they feel something amiss, possibly forbidding, that emanates from the fisher, an energy that drives through arms and hands like a subtle electricity, a current present in the rod and line, an energy field that they wish not to enter. When desire leaves, or the fisher is ready to quit, that field opens up for the fish, or vanishes, and the fish strikes. I realize that I am being unscientific, but my sense of fish behavior is born of lots of time spent (or wasted) fishing.

A fisher does best, of course, in a state of relaxed awareness, or calm alertness. Lose yourself in your surroundings: the sharpness of the air, the soothing sunlight, or the supernatural mist creeping over the stream. Watch the way the fog lingers in the willows, the most joyful of all trees.

Fish School, or Going to School with the Fish

Sometimes it's a good idea to explore a small trout stream before attempting to fish there in order to discover where the fish are, then to return the next day to those sites. I once went on a fish-finding expedition not far from home, in a winding creek called Mill Brook, a stream where people seldom fish, primarily due to the dense brush and the difficulty in finding enough open space on this sinewy stream to cast. The season was early September, and I figured the trout in the bigger streams, the Battenkill and Mettawee, had grown wary and weary of my presence. What I found was that Mill Brook was positively teeming with wild brookies. There were fry, baby fish under a year old, scattered throughout the brook. The fry tend to avoid the open spaces where the more mature fish are because they are more vulnerable to predators, including cannibals.

The winding stream was alive with pools, many about four or five feet wide and a few feet deep, with schools of larger fish, fingerlings, and two and three year olds. (Most species of trout have a life span of seven years, though seldom survive that long.) These pools were thick with fish. Such pools, located in the deep parts of trout streams, are ideal for fish because of their depth, which provides cooler water and greater protection, and, in small streams, space for trout to survive. All sorts of trout food empties into them. In one pool I counted up to sixty fish, and decided that estimating was good enough. Because it was late in the season when water levels are lower, the trout in this creek had clustered, schooled in the safer, deeper pools. But how to get at them without panicking them off; how to cast into their watery classroom? I knew that I could not approach them from the front, from the small current that emptied into the pool, they'd see me, and trout, especially wild trout, will not bite when they see someone fishing for them. Rod in hand, I navigated up the bank, thick with goldenrod and asters and fading pink clusters of Joe-pye weed, circling in behind the pool.

Stepping cautiously into the shallow water, I arrived not ten feet behind the school. The pool was crystal clear, now and then a ripple making a diaphanous film over the surface that clarified in seconds. At first the trout rustled a bit, but then settled down, all sixty or seventy of them

63

facing upstream, their tails lightly waving to keep them in place, packed in tight like a squadron. The bigger trout were up front of the school to get first pick of whatever treats wafted down the current and over a small rock inches above the pool. The largest of the Brookies, who hovered foremost of the school, was about 12 to 14 inches.

There were dead sumac branches hanging partially over the pool, which I snagged on my first cast. I couldn't tug the line free. The best solution was to wade into the pool, and free the fly. I decided to clear away the dead branches to leave room for casting another time. Maybe tomorrow. The fish darted all around me, frantically careering in the pool, while I snapped the dead branches easily and flung them onto the bank. I noticed that most of the fish hadn't shot up or down the creek, but instead streaked back and forth across the pool, so I decided to return to my catbird seat behind them, and watch. As the sand and tiny pebbles settled back to the pool's floor, the fish returned, and did so hastily, as though they couldn't wait for class to resume and get back into formation. The last fish to return to the squadron was the biggest, who came darting down from upstream to reclaim his valedictorian space. Planted silently behind the school, motionless, yet not uncomfortable, I did not fret the trout, which gaze only forward and to their sides.

I cast as far forward as possible to tempt the bigger fish, gradations of size going all the way to the back of the school where the fingerlings were. At first my casts disturbed the water, and the fish, but eventually they all settled in and got accustomed to the soft landings my fly made. This really was fish school for me, as I got to observe them, their behavior regarding my casts and the fly that drifted by. Shortly one took the nymph I was casting. After I unhooked her she returned to her place in the school, as though nothing had happened but detention. My sense is that after you release a trout, they tend to return to the haunt where you have caught them. What was even more interesting was that none of the other fish were disturbed. One would expect that after all the struggle and flailing, the other trout would have panicked out of the pool, but none did. Obviously trout are undisturbed by their partners' capture, perhaps in the same way we ignore those among us returned after alien abductions.

I decided to try dry fly fishing, thinking this pool might be one of those places where dry flying is more effective than wet fly or nymphing. This school did not at all mind me behind them while I knotted a stonefly onto my line. Sure enough, one lunged for the fly before it touched the water. Another snapped my fly and tried to return to her place in the formation with the hook in mouth. I caught three more, but less quickly each time, as though the trout were learning all along. Many, many more trout hit the fly without taking it, each returning to the collective, the other fish reacting to the disturbance the way a flock of pigeons might when one squeezes into the perch, with hardly a rustle. I had great fun watching them strike in the water. Never once did any of the bigger fish up front go for my flies, several types of which I later tried, but none as effective as the stonefly. I wonder yet, what would have worked to tempt those bigger fish up front, which hardly stirred as the flies I cast drifted over their savvy, speckled heads? Of course those big heads got that way not by accident but by being leery and difficult.

Wet Fly, Dry Fly, Nymphs

Bitterness and guilt are inevitable human emotions, but they must be mastered, and fly fishing is an effective way to let go of them. We have all had things happen to us that were cruel and unfair. We have all made mistakes, and I would argue that a life without regrets is a life not lived. We have all done things of which we are not proud. Many of these things cannot be fixed. I like the idea of reaching a state where there is no more time for bitterness and regret. Fishing works for me, and fly fishing works best. Whatever past wrongs done to me, whatever past wrongs I have done, when I am in a stream I know I am living well, and whatever has led me to this fishing life had to happen to get me into this present moment, which I would never want changed and for which I am grateful.

When I first started fly fishing, I wanted to leap immediately into perfection, to fish in the best way, which most perceive as dry fly angling. The desired effect is to make a cast of such exquisiteness that a 20 inch wild rainbow will hit the fly before it even lights on the water. These are rarefied experiences that can and do happen, but unnecessary to delight in fly angling. I still dry fly fish now and then, sometimes I fly wet. Like most fly anglers, I am part instructed, part self-taught. I decided to switch primarily to wet and nymph fly fishing after reading William Humphrey's slender masterpiece, *My Moby Dick*. The book centers around his quest one summer in the Berkshires to capture a gigantic rainbow which he stalked until the final day of fishing season.

One Eye, as he called him, was, like all great fish, a mythic creature which had eluded him all summer, yet Humphrey felt such a fish should only be pursued in the most elite of styles, artistically, to match the fish's grandeur. Hence, dry fly. On that last, fateful day of fishing season, the monster took his fly: "Exploding from the water, the fish took it on the wing, a foot above the surface. Why that cast and none of the countless others, nobody will ever know. Instantly he felt the barb. Not fright, but fight, was what it brought out in him."

Humphrey was dry fly fishing, using a #12 Black Gnat, he tells us. Wet fly fishing is the use of fly patterns that mimic creatures trout feed on subsurface; dry flies imitate those that are winged, found on or just above a stream's surface, and nymphs are those intermediate patterns, masquerading as insects not yet in their full adult stage that have yet to develop wings. Nymphs float a little below the surface, so nymphing is the middle way, intermediate between dry and wet. You might expect the best fly fishers to use all three patterns, depending upon the conditions, season, even time of day, but I think most have a preference, the reasons for which I cannot always tell. I prefer nymphing, casting my lure a little below the surface. I just seem to do better with nymphs. I don't think the reasons are Freudian, nor do they have anything to do with my love for classical mythology. There isn't anything sexually exciting about fly nymphs, nor much aesthetically pleasing about these bizarre-looking objects, though, as in all patterns, there is a certain whimsy to their designs. Nor do I think an in-depth study of my life would provide much of an explanation for my preference.

The best I can offer is this: when I choose a nymph pattern, I am confident I have a good chance of catching something. Therefore I don't have to spend time anguishing about my selection, and can let go of that one particularly distracting thought. I am comfortable with having a nymph floating a little beneath the surface and derive pleasure from catching a trout there, where sometimes I can get a good look at the fish before landing him. My understanding is that trout generally surface feed about 10 percent of the time. Forget about having to dry fly fish to have the best experience. As you are progressively learning, you will catch more fish wet flying or nymphing, but some are simply "called" to dry fly. The preference among the three will simply find you.

As time goes by, I must admit my preference for dry fly angling varies. Let me put it this way: It's more exciting catching a fish wet fly than not catching a fish dry fly. Nevertheless, when dry flying, you can see the fish rise for your lure, take it before you even feel your line pull, and dive back under. For me, this makes dry fly especially exciting. How do you know when dry fly fishing will probably work? If you see trout rising, they'll rise for your dry fly. If you are able, try to figure out what's flying around that the trout are taking, or simply experiment with different classic dry flies like blue winged olives, light cahills, or red quill emergers. You may not necessarily need to match the hatch to get a fish, but your chances improve when you do.

The Milky Way and the Three Thousand Fly Patterns

For angling may be said to be so like the Mathematicks, that it can ne'r be fully learnt.

Izaak Walton, *The Compleat Angler*

I have no more understanding of why there are roughly 3,000 fly patterns, identifying them all a profoundly easier task than identifying the stars in our galaxy, which astronomers estimate at approximately 200 billion, but I am glad for the variety and do not need to know each one of them any more than I need to know the names of all the Milky Way's stars, (most of which will likely remain forever unnamed) to admire their beauty or abundance. If one could know all their names or qualities would one better understand God's mind? Near the end of a long and distinguished career, British naturalist J. B. S. Haldane was questioned by a cleric about his thoughts on the nature of the Creator. In that manner of droll understatement particular to his island, Haldane, referring to the 300,000 known species of Coleoptera, replied that whatever the nature of God, he has "an inordinate fondness for beetles."

In North America there are thousands of species of insects and crustaceans that trout feed on. Fortunately, thousand of species, or should we say sub-species, of fly fishermen have experimented on trout using multiple varieties of fly patterns. You needn't be an entomologist to learn the most effective flies, for you can hone this number down to a few dozen reliable patterns and, if you wish, keep to a dozen or so old standbys for most scenarios. My solution might be reckoned a form of surrender to overwhelming numbers, and it may be. Of the thousands of aquatic species that trout could feed on, ichthyologists seem to agree on the number they prefer: about 1,500. (The traditional estimated number of Zen koans is 1,700.) This figure does not take into account all the variations in size and color, time of day, mood of the fish, the precision of your casts, and all the other sundry, perhaps unknowable, variables present in the underwater world that is entirely alien to us, except, perhaps, in our world of the unconscious. The remedy for the desire to comprehend such a daunting entomology, or to achieve perfection in fly selection, then, may be to embrace the unconscious mind in such a way that it is no longer terra incognita, or mare incognita, to swim inside yourself like a fish while you are fishing.

68

Trout tend to be as wily as the ravens who mock me while I fish. Cautious as crows, more skitterish than the redwing blackbirds who populate the honeysuckles and dogwoods and willows along the banks, more finicky than a movie star's housecats, trout require grace to catch.

I suspect that devotion to learning all the fly patterns and when they work could turn into obsession, making you forget that the great moments in fly fishing are shaped by chance, intuition, and spontaneity. Attempting to learn all or most fly patterns would be the equivalent of wrestling with the medieval question of the scholastics: "How many angels can dance on the head of a pin?" The question is koan-like, with no fixed solution, but functioned to help one envision the infinite, and to realize the impossibility of understanding God. Nevertheless, Saint Columba of Ireland determined that the number of angels that can dance on the head of a pin is 20,000,216. I am not sure of the mathematical formula he used to calculate this number, but admire his faithful tenacity and mad precision.

How many trout are there in the Rivers of Heaven? Perhaps 20,000,216, or thereabouts.

Bats

A fly fisherman I know once told me, poetic intensity in his voice, that the absolute best time for fishing is when it gets dark, not when night falls, necessarily, but right at the very moment of darkness, when the dim, mauve light of dusk vanishes. That is the very instant when fish will bite. He told me of catching a 16 inch wild rainbow at precisely the moment of first darkness.

The danger of fishing in the dusk and dark of late summer is bats. Not that bats are dangerous, unless you decide to handle a sick and dying one, or you stupidly swat at them and get scratched accidentally. Bats will fly perilously close, but their sonar is perfect and they'll never brush you. They fly about eating moths and the mosquitoes that do want to bite you. Unfortunately, hibernating bat species in Northeast have been decimated by White Nose Syndrome, called so because of the whitish mildew that appears on the bats' noses, a bacteria possibly imported from European bats that somehow arrived in the U.S. The disease interrupts bats' hibernating patterns, causing them to wake when the weather is still cold, and thus depleting their energy stored to survive the winter. I don't know how this environmental disaster will play out, but I am hopeful that the bats that do survive the disease will pass on their immunity to their young. The bats in Europe and the British Isles are immune. At any rate, it will take years and years for the populations to recover on their own (if they do) for bats reproduce slowly, usually one pup at a time. There are still bats around, but far fewer, and many more mosquitoes as a result.

The most prevalent bats here in the northeast had been Little Brown Bats and Pipistrelles, a name derived from the Latin for vespers. These tiny brown creatures have bodies only a few inches long, wingspans not much more than six inches. They arrive before dark, weave around only a few feet above the water, feed for a couple of hours, each one eating as many as three thousand moths and mosquitoes in an evening. Their sonar gives them pinpoint accuracy and, contrary to popular belief, they are not blind at all. They all come out together and feast in flight, then all finish together and return to their colony, often in a cave, whence they sometimes emerge later for a midnight snack.

I enjoy their aerial acrobatics. Occasionally their wings will brush your fishing line, but this hurts nothing. The danger is that the bats are curious about your fly and may chase it when you cast. It is easy for them to snatch your fly and flutter off madly while you have to reel the bat back in, as though you have caught a little black flying fish. I regard catching a bat as disastrous because you can't save your fly, and you are harming an ally that might feel physical pain in the way a human does, for bats are mammals. The best thing to do when bats are flickering about is to cease casting and to keep your line in the stream. You can still manipulate your line into places where fish may be, though not nearly as efficiently as when casting.

The little brown bats that are most common in the Northeast, are not to be feared, yet it is unrealistic to expect most people to like them as I do. But I believe that if bats are to recover, part of that recovery entails people changing their attitudes about them.

Friends in my village or nearby sometimes call me when they have a bat in the house. Many people can't help fearing them. There is no need to chase bats out your house with a broom or tennis racquet. The best way to get a bat out is simply to turn off your lights and open the door. I don't mind taking them out of houses for my friends and, like the trout, I catch and release bats. By doing so I get to see them up close, snared in the fish net I use to relocate them, with their wings outspread, their tiny black claws caught, their intelligent, defiant eyes shunning the light. Their faces are gnome-like, and when they open their wings, like capes, in the net, exposing their lewd bodies and long, crooked arms fused to their wings, they look like fallen angels or doll-sized Draculas.

71

The Ones That Get Away, the Sequel

As always there are ones that get away, and there is a concurrent alteration in the fisherman's memory regarding such a fish. The memory gets blurry, and the imagination expands. As a result the size of the fish tends to increase, sometimes dramatically. I know of no good explanation for this phenomenon, except that in the excitement of playing and attempting to land the fish, the fisherman consistently overestimates its size, and therefore, upon reflection, must reassemble a more accurate image of the fish's true size, which grows larger with the passage of time. The more gender specific term *fisherman* is more appropriate in this case because female fishers seem to be free of this widespread male malady wherein memory and perception are severely distorted and, because size sometimes matters, might even be prone to exaggerate. No one, at any rate, boasts about how tiny the fish was that he caught.

Wild estimations about lunkers and monsters, even if they are inaccurate, should give little disturbance to the fly angler. Memory, like time and space, is elusive. If you happen to over estimate the size of your escaped fish, it is unlikely anyone will be concerned. For some reason the veracity of fishermen is often questioned, so you should not be concerned if few people believe you almost landed a two foot rainbow.

Cell Phones, Wrist Watches and Herman Melville

"So long as one is conscious of space and time, Zen will keep a respectable distance from you," wrote D. T. Suzuki, the Japanese scholar who devoted much of his life to helping Westerners understand Zen. Leave your cell phone home, or at least in your car. Yes, you may die of a stroke in the stream, or break a leg and drown, a current taking you where only fish and other aquatic creatures live. A trout may pull you under, and take you too far to ever return, or you may get zapped by lightning, but the stream's a better place to die than most. The purpose of fly angling is to enter another world by breaking habitual ways of looking at things. Not that *this world* is illusory or unreal, but that our experience of it is obscured through the filter of ego-consciousness, which includes our own particular way of experiencing time and space. Just as we often cannot see the living trout blended beneath the surface, a more shimmering world is hidden within our consciousness of time and space. For means of survival, we cannot always dwell in that world, but fly angling can allow us to visit.

While in that world that belongs as much, if not more, to the fish people as us, leave your watch behind, lose the phone, get lost in the stream. Iphones (is there irony here, that which keeps you connected to your I?) and wrist watches, by the way, attract lightning. When casting and focused on catching fish, this single-mindedness of attention gives the mind, and body, a relaxed keenness seldom to be found in other forms of exercise. The fisher forgets all else. For me, this is as fine as any yoga or meditation. Yet, there is another, maybe equally raptured state one sometimes slips into by watching the water for long intervals. Herman Melville in *The Mast-Head* chapter of *Moby Dick* writes of sailors whose job it was to watch for whales:

"[B]y the blending cadence of waves with thoughts, that at last he loses his identity; takes the mystic ocean at his feet for the visible image of that deep, blue, bottomless soul, pervading mankind and nature; and every strange, half-seen, gliding, beautiful thing that eludes him; every dimly discovered, uprising fin of some indiscernible form, seems to him the embodiment of those elusive thoughts that only people the soul by continually flitting through it. In this enchanted mood, thy spirit ebbs away to whence it came, becomes diffused through time and space."

73

We should all of us pay a visit now and then to that place whence our spirit comes. Melville warns mariners who are of dreamy or poetic nature of the danger to be mesmerized into such a reverie that they will fall from their crow's nest. An advantage to reaching such a state in a trout stream is that the threat of drowning or falling isn't much. To be awakened from your reverie with a fish on is fine, and I've often been yanked out of a reverie by a tugging trout, but it's better to be ready for one, and more than once have traded a trout for a daydream.

Big Fish, Small Fish

One midsummer evening, when all around the Battenkill hung gray, heavy, humid air, although wading in the Kill itself was cool and pleasant--another fisherman came splashing around the bend where I was casting for Browns. We said our hellos, he asked, "How far up river is Pook's Bridge?" But he was clearly irritated, barking as he stomped up the bank, "I'd rather catch one big one than a shitload of little ones."

Just how much would a shitload be? Clearly he meant ten or twenty fish, though I now believe that a shitload could comprise a minimum of eight fish. What size is little? Where does little end and medium begin? What is the transitional stage between fire and smoke? Did a middle size exist for this fishermen, or was his world two dimensional, consisting of only big and little? At what size can we call a trout big?

According to the brochure *Fish Vermont* published by the Vermont Fish and Wildlife Department, the average size of browns is 8 to 18 inches. Brookies sometimes called square tails) are listed at 6 to 12, and rainbows average 7 to 8 inches. Certainly there are bigger trout of all three species, but if you catch a 10 inch Rainbow, you've done great. The fallacy that you can only have a good time catching monsters has dampened the amount of joy many have fishing. I believe fishermen themselves are responsible for the misconception; fly anglers are notorious in their inclinations to lie, or, as fishermen like to put it, exaggerate. Perhaps in this age of genetic discovery scientists will find a chromosomal relationship between attraction to fishing and the propensity to lying, at least among males.

How often does one hear a fly fisher boast of catching an 8 inch brook trout? If you are using a light-weight fly rod, and rid yourself of trophy-sized expectations, and fish isolated in clandestine brooks and streams, bringing in an 8 inch brook trout is a thrill. Trout are fierce little fish, amazingly strong. If you don't get a rush from playing and landing an 8 incher, either your tackle is too heavy or desire is obstructing your line.

Beyond Work and Play

When I am in a trout stream I feel as though what I am doing (which is both close to nothing yet infinitely different from nothing) is exactly what I am supposed to be doing, what I was born to do. This might sound bizarre to those for whom work, career, duty, and responsibility form the locus of life's activities.

Primitive cultures (*primitive* in the superior sense of being in touch with the body and the natural world and recognizing no mind-body split) teach us much when we pay them attention. They've taught us, for one thing, to redefine primitive as a style of art, a type of living that is as richly complex as technologically "advanced" cultures, but not nearly as complicated. A life infused with imagination, wildness, humor, primitive cultures exemplify lifestyles in which sharing reduces everyone's work. Any carpenter knows that with a helper a house will be built not twice as fast but many times faster, that two carpenters with two helpers will build maybe sixteen times faster. Those in primitive cultures have known and lived this fact of communal labor for millennia. Often the dichotomy of work and play does not exist. There is play in work, which many of us no longer know, and work in play, which perhaps more of us do know. And then there is fishing. Admittedly, I embrace technologic improvements in fly angling, but those improvements are largely founded on the older, primitive designs. Every once in a while I get the urge to use one of my old bamboo rods and, though I prefer the lighter graphite models, I never experience a twinge of regret having fished with the old bamboo.

No Problem Zen

I once believed the true Zen angler didn't care if he caught fish, was more interested in the lightness of the fly rod, and the perfection of the cast. I was wrong. There is nothing like catching a trout while fishing with a light rod. But to desire too much interferes with the fishing. A conundrum. What does an angler do? The Zen fisher does everything necessary to lure a trout, then focuses to the point of disappearance of self. This happens naturally. The self cannot will itself to vanish. Such a disappearance only happens through joyful distraction.

When a trout is suddenly on, the self does not return. You are the no one who is playing and landing that trout. You are nothing else, no one else. All the rest is briefly lost in the thrill. That such a loss is temporary, is integral to our survival. We're not here long. Any practicing of loss of self that is joyful and invigorating is good practice for the final time when we let go of this world. Catch and release.

Within or Without the Nightmare

The world is a waking nightmare. Little children are burned to death in tenement fires in the South Bronx, or they step onto landmines in Cambodia. Powerful nations spend trillions on "defense" but mere millions on poverty. Open spaces are ruined for "development," garbage is everywhere. We are living in the midst of a mass extinction and, if we fail to step from the brink we are fast approaching, we may make this celestial jewel on which we live uninhabitable for future generations. Yet, somehow, there is not only room in this world for joy, but because that joy is real, we know another side to human suffering. Those who know happiness, who are able "to eat their grief joyfully," as poet Robert Bly once said, show us one way out of the nightmare. Without joy, we are no good; we are but a burden to others. I refuse to feel guilty about wasting my life fishing. If your guilt weighs more than you, you can't be a Zen fisher. I believe you can lose your guilt by loving this world, and doing what you love. Perhaps this is a trite philosophy, but it's what I believe.

Mulligan's Comet

The universe is an optical illusion. The earth appears to be flat, but it's spherical. The sun appears to rotate around the earth, but the earth rotates around the sun. Starlight seems spontaneous, but all of it was emitted deep in the past. The wind driving the clouds at night makes the moon fly. All artists are illusionists. Fly tyers are also illusionists. Fish illusionists. Fly tying is a whimsical, if not strange, calling. Rather than quibbling over whether fly tying is a craft or an art, we can at least call it a practice that has elements of art and craft, possibly science also. Some fly tyers, whose special talent is making fishing lures, do not fish, the most celebrated of whom was the Scottish tyer Megan Boyd, who feared causing pain for trout and salmon, and whose flies are regarded as masterpieces. There is something of an artist-mad scientist fusion in the obsessive fly tyer at work in the basement workshop, or laboratory.

Suppose a mad fly tyer were to make a fish hypnotizer that he dubbed Mulligan's Comet. Suppose the brilliance of the fly were not that trout would pursue it, but that they would marvel at it as it streaked through the water, marvel in such a way that whatever next fly comes along, they strike. They strike because Mulligan's Comet generates in the fish a hunger for the sky in the same way that we are drawn to water. Of course every lure they are lunging for is an illusion, and so much of what they like falls from the sky, or, at least, hovers briefly over the stream.

Spiders

There are several small streams I like to fish in. The Mettawee River and the Indian River both, like small streams, are narrow, with lots of overhanging brush. White Creek, Camden Creek, and Mill Brook are also my favorites. The banks are thick with willow trees, red twig dogwood, and honeysuckle, which flower in May. Because all is closer, more intimate in smaller steams, perspective is different. The birds are closer, as are their nests. Orioles and yellow warblers in spring, always Red-winged blackbirds, singing, or fussing. Often amid the tangle of twigs over the stream are spider webs. One looks at a spider differently, her net woven in such a precarious spot.

These webs are spun by fishing spiders, who use nets to catch their prey, not hunting spiders like wolf spiders or wood spiders. How strange the same world as ours is for them. The rushing stream dappled with sunlight must be like a cataract of light and flood. Tiny insects that are born in water, emerge in their adult stage as winged, swarming above the stream. Like mayflies, spinners and caddis flies, emergers comprise hundreds of species of flying creatures that trout like to eat, as do spiders.

Among the finest sights a fly fisher can witness on a morning stream, with the mist like smoke afloat over the water, are the spider webs that appear everywhere in late summer. Dew-laden, the webs are visible only in the morning, festooning the deadfall over the creek like the rigging of shipwrecks.

Spiders are monstrous. Eight legs, butt fused to torso, little bald head grotesquely affixed, eight lidless eyes, fangs instead of mouth. Wicked things that keep the world in balance. And when a spider catches that deer fly that's been pestering you, she weaves it in silk and paralyzes it. She takes repeated feedings from her captive, sucking out its vital juices, drinking it alive, so to speak. The most horrific monsters on earth, excluding humans, are fortunately tiny.

In the natural world, perspective and proportion are critical. Imagine if we were pygmy-sized, pygmies being thirteen inches tall according to the ancient Greeks, the calculation based on arm's length from wrist to elbow. Spider bites and bee stings would kill us. Mosquitoes would be larger than ospreys. Trout would be hunted like whales. Thoughts in the smaller streams are carried to unusual places. How perfect are the proportions of things. How miraculous the tiny. With a light-weight fly rod, a six-inch wild brook trout, spinning frantically out of the water with his spots aglitter in the sunlight, is a great catch. Often such fish struggle so wildly that they unhook themselves and I only get a quick glance at them as I hold them briefly out of the water. And when they hit the stream, they vanish so quickly one might think they evaporate, or disappear supernaturally.

The Demon of Self-Irony

The satisfactions of a day's fishing are deep; and just as deep on a day when you don't catch a fish; but unless you keep faith that you are going to catch a fish that day, then fishing seems a waste–a waste of time, money, effort, and, most depressing, a waste of spirit. Faith and faith alone can guard the fisherman against a demon of which he is particularly the prey, the demon of self-irony, from acquiescence in the opinion of the ignorant that he is making a fool of himself.

The Spawning Run, William Humphrey

We all star in our own movies, sometimes compressed, sometimes epic, sometimes tragic, sometimes comedic. The trick is to realize that not only we are starring (and maybe directing), but in the movies of others we co-star, or have roles as incidental characters, or merely make cameo appearances. We make this realization by being self-reflective, stepping outside of ourselves. But this same self-reflectiveness, so necessary to living well, to understanding and feeling for others, can be dangerous. We could be absurd, living a vain tragi-comedy.

Rather than the "Fool on the Hill," you could be the Fool in the River. Maybe there are no fish where you're fishing, and you are the only one who doesn't know. If you allow the demon of doubt to overtake you, you'll start behaving clumsily. Your casting will become oafish. Impatience will take away your focus, which will prevent you from catching fish. The problem won't be failure to catch fish, but will instead be failure to have fun trying. When I am fishing well I am not worried about making money, or achieving power, or impressing others. I am not saddened that others do not know how liberating this experience is, that it is repeated again and again, but in each way new. I care only about raising a creature of beauty out of the water, and if that creature isn't a mermaid, well then, a trout is good enough.

Today I am in the Mettawee. From the road where I parked I followed a little feeder brook until I reached the silver span that suddenly appeared around the brook's bend. I struggled upriver until I passed a few deep pools where I could fish my way back. These deep pools are tricky, draped with dead fall, but they are deep and light green and perfect hiding places for rainbows. I knot a flashback hare's ear and cast. It

82

floats into the pool, and I am careful to control the line so that the current doesn't snap it on the branches under the water. This is risky, but worth the trouble. In moments the rod bends. Who'd have thought such a powerful force lives in that little, swirling spring pool cascaded with a barricade of sunken willow branches? I bring the trout spangling out of the water, still writhing defiantly as I rest my rod on the bank. He's off the hook before my fingers even reach his jaw.

Dry Flying

Much has been written about the merits of dry, wet, streamer (a form of wet fly that resemble minnow shapes), or nymph angling. Although trout, like all fish, are primarily sub-surface feeders, the conclusion that your odds of catching fish are greatly increased by shunning the dry fly is sometimes faulty. The truth is that when you get good at fly fishing, your odds of catching trout are often better dry fly, depending upon all sorts of conditions like weather, time of day, and the prevailing hatch. If you know how to locate where the fish are, use stealth skillfully, and are able to cast with fineness and accuracy, and, finally, your pattern or fly selection is good, you can often catch more trout dry fly than the other ways.

The hang-up seems to be fly selection, but there are about a dozen patterns that most always work, so if you are willing to experiment, and change flies when one isn't getting much of a response, you don't need to learn hundreds upon hundred of hatches to figure out what the fish will take on such and such time during the first week of July, or during an overcast dusk in August, or to keep a log of daily catches on what fly and in what conditions. Keeping a log can be fun, and provide you with a history of adventures, like a sea captain, but it should be done more for your enjoyment. When you dry fly, you can often see the trout take your pattern. The fish rise for you.

Charybdis

In *The Odyssey* Charybdis destroys Odysseus' ship and crew. Charybdis is a monster in the shape of a giant whirlpool. The spring pools in trout streams are quite beautiful, but sometimes perilous. The current that flows into the spring pool forms a whirlpool, quite charming to the eye, infinitesimally smaller than Charybdis. These pools are frequent and could be called the Charybdisids, or the children of Charybdis, because of the danger they can pose. A spring pool is not a pool that occurs in the spring time. A spring pool is simply a spring that is under the stream, that creates eddies, and these springs are often a vital part of a stream's water supply. Trout love spring pools.

The woody debris that gathers along the edges of these pools and the deep water within them provide excellent habitat and shelter for trout, but they must be fished with prudence. If your fly gets lost in one of these pools, which can easily occur, it may be best to forego retrieving it, else you might drown like one of Odysseus' men.

Chub

My first several years fly fishing I'd occasionally catch feisty little fish that I mistook for trout. Chub look almost identical to trout, share pools and streams with them in harmony, fight just as hard, and strike at the same flies. Some anglers like to call them white fish, but they are another species altogether. The more accurate name for this fish is Smelt (Osmerus mordax). The only visible difference between trout and chub (or smelt), as far as I can determine, is coloration and size. Smelt are generally small and have none of the exotic coloration of trout. They are shaped identically, at least the kind I've been catching in the northeast, but are scaly and of a radiant, silver color. There doesn't seem to be a lot of information on them, perhaps because "chub" is a generic term for several different species. These species are in the cyprinoid family, generally small, soft-finned fishes with cycloid (circular or arranged in circles) scales. The types of fish often called chub include fallfish, horned dace, golden shiner, squawfish, hornyhead, and several different species of salt water fish. In some regions, black bass and lake heron are called chub. Identifying fish can be confusing. There are an estimated 25,000 species of fish on the planet, mostly salt water, with new species discovered each year.

In obsolete slang, a chub is a dolt, a fool, a lout, a dullard, or spiritless person. I guess nowadays a chub would be someone far overweight. Such a one would have trouble catching chub, which are often in small streams and almost as tricky as trout. What exact species of chub I've been catching I've no idea, and although most are small, around six inches, I've occasionally caught some that grow large, one about fourteen inches in the Adirondacks. I'm just glad to catch whatever I can. After all, a fish is a fish, and catching any kind is a thrill. Any angler who expresses disappointment at failing to land the fish they are after is, as far as I'm concerned, a chub.

Waterfalls

In some trout streams you'll find waterfalls. There is one I like to fish in where the falls drop about 15 feet or more. I don't recommend fishing off the falls, but under them. Not directly under them. There is a presence in waterfalls one can only know by standing under or near them for a while, though one who has any imagination whatsoever recognizes that presence immediately. It is as though the crashing of the falls drowns out the white noise inside the mind and replaces that void with its own voice, or voices. The cataract enters the mind and replaces it with many voices that speak as though enthralled. And this language is a speech that is just out of reach of any words or human tongue. The translation of the waterfall's babble must be made by the hearer at the time, and what one hears can never be recounted verbatim, or even roughly, though one remembers an ecstatic quality about the fall's diction.

The falls to fish in are those that spill into spring pools that are five feet, ten feet or even deeper, where the swirling eddies prevent you from seeing the bottom, and obscure you from the fishes' sight. If trout see you, they will never bite. The falls spill a white tongue into green pools of bubbling water. Not far beneath that erupting water are sometimes trout. Such pools often teem with them, not directly beneath, but around the margins.. Get over to where you can cast into the pool below the falls. Sometimes the falls will lead down into a flume, a narrow passageway in the rocks the fast moving water has carved over millennia. I have caught rainbow trout in these cold water flumes.

When angling below falls don't worry if the eddy carries your fly down deep. That's what you want. There is a rapturous excitement when trawling for fish this way, pulling one out, struggling with both the fish and the pool's currents, the fall's spray misting the light, and you understand why a fish would dwell near such a place. For a trout there must be a sense of complete safety in such an inaccessible deep where predators cannot reach.

Fly Fishing Fashion

A small stream fly fisher is a minimalist. Lighter is better in fishing, and maybe most everything else, too. The fly rod should weigh under two ounces, be less than eight feet long, preferably less than seven. The reel should be light-weight. Fishing line should be four-weight, or under, down even to one-weight. It is also best to be minimalist about one's fishing clothes and gear, but exactly what is necessary and what is superfluous? There is nothing in-and-of-itself wrong with wearing waders or hip boots, but such heavy gear can weigh you down. If it's summer time, which, after all, is the best time of the year to fish for trout, all you really need is a T-shirt, swimming trunks, and wading boots, or even old sneakers. You cannot ignore the danger that deer ticks pose, so it's best to spend more time in the water than on the stream banks. I, for one, consider Deet mostly harmless to humans. Any scientist since Paracelsus knows that toxicity is in dosage, not in substance. A good home remedy insect repellant is vegetable oil. Lather it on. No insect wants to land or crawl onto the stuff. You'll manage to repel everything but your dog, and I don't think the fish have any sense of it.

Fly fishers don't need creels because they practice catch-and-release. It's wise to don a fishing hat if you're susceptible to sunburn, or sunglasses if the sun's glare is too much. I for one feel that sunglasses tend to obscure what one sees. But eye protection is necessary, not simply from the sun but from errant casts. Also, polarized sunglasses work well, and help you to see under the water. Need I say more about cell phones and wrist watches? How about the fact they attract lightning? A light fishing vest will carry all the paraphernalia you should need: fly boxes, fishing license (if you aren't an outlaw), water bottle, bandana, spare leader and tippet lines, snips and zinger, knife, band aids, insect repellent, sunscreen, tape measure (for the monster you'll land), eyeglasses that you are not afraid of losing or breaking, and a lucky talisman. (One day you'll find that talisman in the stream while you are fishing. You'll recognize it, him, or her when you see it. Mine is a squat, three inch plastic cowboy in a Stetson with a detachable lasso. I saved him from oblivion in the Battenkill.)

Why fish light? The more one carries, the more one is burdened. It's like owning things. Eventually your stuff starts to own you. Often I see guys in full fly fishing regalia, and though they may appear photogenic or just right for an idyllic Field and Stream cover, I am not sure they are always comfortable. Such fishers look screwed in, or anchored to the spot they're fishing from. I like to be able to move up and down stream, to visit different sites. You can only fish in a spot for so long until the fish grow wary, dismissing even the most elegant of fly patterns as common frauds, bored and immovable as the most spoiled fish princesses at the ball. I understand that some of us are younger or more athletic, but the more you balance yourself in the water, trudge across the currents and wade the streams, the more you are able to do so. Agility is not simply a gift of nature, but must be nurtured.

Fighting Fish

In chapter XXXII of Genesis Jacob wrestles with an angel all night long. At daybreak Jacob refuses to release the angel until he blesses him, which the angel does. Afterwards, his hip injured, Jacob declares that he has seen the face of God. I know nothing of the range of interpretations of this story, but obvious to me is that to gain wisdom, to experience illumination or some form of revelation, is not easily had. One must struggle, like a fish, or a fisher. Perhaps this is the reason the angel injures Jacob's thigh. Not that pain must be involved in the attainment of illumination, but to "initiate" Jacob in some way, to reveal that what he is wrestling with has extraordinary power. The angel merely "touched...the hollow of Jacob's thigh" (his hip?) in order to cause him injury. When dawn arrives, and the angel finally cries uncle, Jacob will not relent until the angel blesses him. Surely the divine being could have kicked Jacob's butt, but some test (Yahweh is a stickler for trials and exams) is occurring, including the condition that Jacob has to fight injured. Where the angel has touched him, and where they have fought, become sacred, yet Jacob cannot coax out the angel's name. Why does the angel refuse this information? Some theologians conclude that the angel is God. Must something always remain unknown, or ineffable?

I think most anglers would agree that it is better to have a good hard fight attempting to land a trout and losing that fish at the last second, just when you've reeled it out of the water, than to have an easy fight and actually land your fish. Every fly angler should intuitively understand the story of Jacob and his wrestling bout with the nameless angel, because every angler must know the zest of a good tangle with a feisty wild brown that's still flipping and fighting even as you're trying to release the fly.

The struggle needn't be long. In fact it probably shouldn't be. If the fish is still wriggling frantically when you've raised it out of the water, still fighting even out of the water, that's best. It's better for the fly fisher to be exhausted rather than the fish. Quickly unhook him while admiring the orange and blue haloes that cover his sides. Don't touch his gills. Don't squeeze him. Don't remove any of his slimy coating. Toss, or better, submerge him back and watch as he darts off like a being that flies.

Fish Rising

In what is arguably the greatest of all fishing stories, Herman Melville displays great artistry, and probably pleasure, describing Moby Dick breaching: "Rising with the utmost velocity from the furthest depths, the sperm whale thus booms his entire bulk into the pure element of air, and piling up a mountain of dazzling foam, shows his place to the distance of seven miles and more...the White Whale tossed himself salmon-like to heaven...Shrouded in a thin drooping veil of mist, it hovered for a moment in the rainbowed air; and then fell swamping back into the deep."

One of the problems in quoting from Melville, and *Moby Dick* in particular, is you can go on indefinitely until you've recopied much of the tome. I wonder if Melville ever fly fished? I suspect he may have seen and fished for brook trout during his years in the Berkshires. Maybe he fished during his boyhood summers in rural upstate New York at his grandfather's place in Gansevoort. And the fact that trout leap, sometimes even before your line has gone taut, is one of the great joys of angling. There is also little danger of a trout drowning you. Of course rainbow trout, the most avid of leapers, had not been transplanted to streams in the east until the 1870's or thereabouts.

A July day in a spring pool in Little White Creek I had a feisty one on: rising suddenly from the crystalline pool, the rainbow trout flung his entire 12 inches into the pure element of air, and casting a wake of sparkling bubbles, breached whale-like to heaven, hovered briefly in the iridescent air, and then plunged with hectic abandon back into the creek.

Small Mouths

A popular misconception is that fly fishing is only for trout. I like to fish for small mouth bass, which are sometimes in the same rivers as trout, living, as near as I can tell, in harmony. I caught my first small mouths fly fishing in the brook behind my brother's property in Litchfield County, Connecticut. Connecticut has literally thousands of small brooks that are largely ignored and harbor wild fish.

The fact is that bass make a great alternative to trout fishing. The bass grow to good size, and even the little ones fight as tenaciously as trout will. The techniques you use are often the same. Dry fly works well, so do streamers like woolly buggers. The best lures are called poppers. They are brightly colored with many legs, large for a fly, with bodies that resemble nothing in nature, unless there is such an aquatic creature that is a cross between a frog, a beetle, and a spider, that is tri-colored in any combinations of white, green, red, orange, blue, and black. Small mouth bass, unlike trout, face in all different directions, so they are harder to sneak up on. But they are also less afraid and will grow accustomed to your presence in the water, and are much more aggressive feeders. So I believe they are easier to catch. Like rainbow trout, they struggle with wild abandon and leap out of the water. Small mouths have a fluorescent green color. Most of the ones I catch are between 8 and 12 inches long, yet certainly they can get larger. Their tongues look much like human tongues, though they are white instead of pink. I suppose they are called small mouth because the shape of their jaw is smaller than other bass species. In the northeast August seems to be the best month to fish for small mouths. Playing a small mouth on a fly rod is great fun. Not only do they fly out of the water, but they are hardy fish. Never have I released a small mouth and wondered if it would survive the struggle.

Practice and Spontaneity

Inspiration, the breathing in of something beyond the ordinary and habitual, is real, but inspiration is not enough to make a great work of art, in the same way that luck is often not enough to catch a fish. In this way, fly fishing shares characteristics with other art forms.

Whether the art form is calligraphy, poetry, dance, music, or fly fishing, disciplined practice is necessary in order to achieve spontaneity. You can experience the same inspiration as Paganini or Shakespeare, and I am convinced many of us do, but if you haven't been practicing, the inspiration will go for naught. Inspiration should not be equated with skill. Luck's visitations, or those of providence, will be less frequent without the skill to take advantage of their emergences. Whenever I am fishing, I am practicing. Performance and practice fuse in fly angling. So while you are practicing, you are actually doing it. The so-called performance is spontaneous, unique, unrecorded, and evanescent.

Dead Streams

Like all fly fishers, I have favorite streams, but it's unwise to visit them too often, because you'll begin expecting things, and lose the joy of surprise. Through habitual looking rather than seeing (even the same form or place is constantly changing when one sees), the beauty of the fishing site will disappear into the ordinary. A stream can become dead because you stop seeing it, realizing it as new. Or a stream can be dead because it is without fish. Therefore, part of the adventure for me is to always search out new brooks and creeks to try my luck in.

Once in these searches I came upon a dead stream, the Green River in Sandgate, Vermont. The river meanders crystal clear under bridges through farmlands, meadows, woods, ringed with beauty. But there were no fish. The water was good and cold, high for early August. The banks were stable, covered in dogwood, willow saplings, grape vines, honeysuckle, raspberry canes. There was plenty of dead fall, deep spring pools, trees overhanging the pools, riffles, swift currents. But no fish. No minnows, no fry, no fingerlings. A strange loneliness crept into me for this ghost river.

There can be only one of three explanations for the dearth of trout: either I am wrong in my observation (certainly not at all outside the realm of possibility); all the fish were poisoned by some form of pollutant and, even if the river is now clean again, the population has not yet been replenished; the river has been over-fished by anglers who do not practice catch-and-release (though it's hard to imagine that the entire trout population could have been obliterated in this manner); or finally some combination of the final two or three has occurred. No true fisher is complacent about this experience. The fisher becomes active with his local fishing or environmental chapter. Conservation efforts require patience, but they work. All fishermen and fisherwomen, no matter their backgrounds, have much to offer in the way of conservation efforts, whether they be fundraising, stream monitoring and testing, writing, organizing, or cleaning trash from the banks and the stream.

I have since visited the Green River, but have, in my admittedly non-scientific observations, seen few fish, and these have mostly been where the river converges with the Battenkill. Strange for a river that appears as though it should be thick with trout. In future summers I will return to see if fish numbers are rising, or if I can discover an answer to the mystery.

Fishing without a Net

Nets can get expensive, and I seldom see the need for one if you're practicing catch-and-release (unless you are landing lunkers with some regularity). The need for a creel is also eliminated. Once you've reeled in a trout and landed it, you're going to have to lay down your fly rod to release the fly from the fish anyway, so why not maneuver the catch onto the shoreline, or wade over to the stream bank, where you can place your rod, then unhook the fish on the bank or just out of the water? Admittedly, landing large fish requires a net, and big river fishing where you'll catch lunkers requires one, but if you are fishing in small streams the largest fish you'll probably catch are going to be about a foot long, and seldom more than a pound. Traveling as light as possible is the best way to fish, even more so when angling in small streams, and a net can get in the way. Also, having a small to mid-sized trout in the net just complicates the process, and you run the risk of getting the fly line all tangled up in the netting. When unhooking a fish, it's easier if the net isn't in the way. Except for those rare times when trying to land a monster, I never understood the net's advantage, particularly when you're not keeping the fish, until I started ocean fishing from a kayak. Because the fish are large, and will disappear into the boat once unhooked, a net is an important tool. But as for angling in mountain brooks, nets are unnecessary and encumbering.

Once you've landed your fish, you can keep it in the water while unhooking it, or, if it's necessary to handle the fish, first dip your hands into the water, thereby making it less likely you'll remove any of the moist coating the trout needs for its survival.

Drag

Drag is the bane of all fly fishers. At least, if you read any books about the practice, you would certainly conclude so. I always had a dim sense of what drag meant, but I made the mistake of assuming that drag signified something specific, some particular error in the way the lure moves on the water to make fish avoid it. Drag is referred to so often in fly fishing articles and books that one would think it's as familiar and universal as the common cold, in no need of explanation, but like the common cold (whatever the common cold is—an ever-mutating virus, whatever a virus is), little is prescribable as a cure for drag.

Thus far I have succeeded, like countless other writers of fly angling books, in writing about drag without really saying what it is. Drag is any unnatural motion of your lure on or underneath the water's surface. The causes of drag are the conditions of the stream, currents for example, the length or thickness of the leader line, the weight of the lure, sloppy or awkward casts. The cures for drag involve paying close attention to the stream's behavior, and adjusting any of the problems aforementioned. One of the reasons so many experts recommend casting upstream is that the flow of the current is more likely to carry your lure downstream in a natural manner, whereas casting downstream is more likely to cause drag once your line tightens, unless you strip out more line, something I like to do.

So, what's the big deal with drag? Well, what's natural, and what isn't? If you cast a fly into a pool, its lack of movement can be just as unnatural as if you retrieve it too quickly, or your twitching motion is bizarre to the fish somehow. Trout, too, can be quirky. What might be natural or inviting to one fish may not necessarily attract another. Then again, what may attract a particular fish at one time of day or year or temperature may not interest that same fish at all on another occasion. Simply stated, sometimes drag may be in the eye of the beholder, and interpreting drag as a reason for not luring fish to your fly may be one means of correcting the problem.

What I am alluding to is that the vagaries of the behavior of fish (let's call them the fish people, even though they are as alien to us as creatures from another galaxy), particularly the trout people, are what can lead us to experimentation and openness. Fly fishing is not an exact science, but a practice, an adventure. My most frequent times of "committing" drag occur when I cast downstream. I used to be in the habit of letting the line go tight, thus my fly, let's say a Gold-ribbed Hare's Ear for example, would remain strangely suspended in the stream in a manner that probably seldom happens in nature. Despite the drag-like behavior of the fly, I might still catch a fish for any number of reasons: one, the fish was hungry and the oddness didn't outweigh his hunger; two, he was an anomalous fish, an oddball among his kind; three, the strangely suspended Hare's Ear fly did in fact behave like something that occurs in the underwater world in rare instances; four, the stream or I momentarily and unconsciously altered motion for a split second enough to make the fly behave naturally; five, the local genii of the river felt sorry for me and impelled the trout to take my lure. Not holding tight, letting go a bit, giving out more line, often gets a trout to strike when you're fishing downstream.

Is Fly Fishing an Art (Or Just a Complicated Way to Goof Off)?

Fly fishing, like Zen, is not tranquilization. It raises my hackles, and not those inert charms in my fly box, when someone remarks that fly angling must be relaxing. Yet I suppose it is relaxing for some, maybe even for me sometimes. The mind clarifies via the sweetness of the wind and water and the repetitions of casting, but one enters into a state of proneness, as a cat will remain for hours near a mouse hole. This is not what I would call relaxing, at least not in the way one naps in a hammock. Keeping one's balance for hours in a trout stream is not relaxation in any conventional sense. One can and should be comfortable when angling, but the comfort is dynamic. The body is quietly active, as is the mind, yet fully active, fully engaged in the activity of fly fishing. Once you have chosen your fly and cast it, presented it in the location in the stream where you believe a fish will grab, there is no longer any need for reason. There is nothing to think about.

Is fly fishing recreation? In that it gets your mind off of things that are taxing, that you need to temporally escape from, perhaps it is. Just to play with the word a bit, fly fishing is not re-creation because each fishing experience is unique and cannot be recreated. For this reason it's not a craft. Nor is the fly fisher recreated. That too would suggest some form of repetition. Casting is repetitive, but only repetitive in the sense of performing a musical piece. Some form of slight variation is inevitable and welcome. There is renewal of sort, but the renewal lies in seeing things differently, which in turn makes them different. Renewal doesn't mean refreshing yourself in order to return to your old habitual self that will need recreating again, as though you were a clone in need of an annual tune up.

The approach to fly fishing can be, and often is, scientific, though functioning as only a science would make the activity artless, and maybe even useful, which would ruin the practice. The power of fly angling is precisely in its uselessness. One fishes for fish (or fun), not truth. Science, what used to be called Natural Philosophy, seeks to understand the physical world through hypothesis and experiment. The fly fisher may apply scientific methods, but isn't out to prove theories on the workings of the *external* universe. The fly fisher comes to understand the interchangeable qualities of the external and internal, that those are concepts circumscribed by words, limited terms for describing limited perception. Fly fishers are of all types of spiritual persuasions; some are atheists, some inclined toward pantheism, so I don't think one can accurately call fly fishing a religion. Fly fishers aren't looking for God in the waters. They are looking for little gods, or Big Trout.

Fly fishing is a sport. But the amount of gracefulness required to practice this sport well makes the term fall short of the mark. One would never call ballet a sport because there is no game involved. Surely there is a goal of performance, of entertaining an audience, of doing one's best, or of catching a fish, but all of this involves a seamlessness. Catching a fish, and releasing it, holding the creature carefully upstream to regain oxygen through the gills, then watching it flutter away or dart off like a phantom, is also part of the art. What's most unusual about the art of fly fishing is that the artist herself is the sole receiver of the aesthetic experience. Strange though it is, I often feel that I'm not the only one when I am fishing. The banks, the trees, the fish, the river and air itself, and something more, others more, are engaged. Attention does not simply lie within oneself.

Most people seem to take for granted that describing fly angling as an art is appropriate, but why? Maybe because art can be used broadly, as in Elizabeth Bishop's poem, "One Art." Perhaps people are prone to calling fly fishing an art because they too have an idyllic picture in their minds. Maybe they've seen fishers in the water casting as though performing sacraments. Perhaps anything with mystique falls loosely into the category of art. For certainly fly fishing is the least efficient method of catching fish and, if indeed an art form, it is among the strangest of such for there is no rehearsal, no completed creation, no audience but for the trout and birds. There is no finished poem or novel to read. No painting or sculpture to see, no music to hear, no dance to watch. In this solitary art form there are only the clouds overhead, and sometimes even they are not present, which is even better.

If I can liken river fly fishing to creating large oil paintings, then let's say small stream fly angling is like making small watercolors. Or better yet, like mandala sand painting, which is also ephemeral. Yet, for me, there is something pretentious about calling fly fishing an art form. Art, craft, science, sport, none of these seem quite right. What strikes me as most accurate is to call fly fishing a practice. Practice is the term used in Zen, meditation, and yoga. Practice unpretentiously covers all the aspects: sport, art, craft, science. And, surely, fly angling demands practice.

Dragons, Damsels and Darners

I live near the Adirondacks, an enormous park, six million acres, rich with myriads of brooks, creeks, rivers and lakes to fish. Today I'm in a kayak on Fourth Lake, catching perch and pan fish, mostly bluegills, with a Woolly Bugger. I am fishing near water's edge, not far from the deadfall and lily pads, where lots of fish shelter. I don't know about other fly anglers, but I like catching pan fish with a light-weight rod. Pan fish are easy to catch with streamers and nymphs, especially beadhead nymphs, and put up a fairly good fight. They are also plentiful and beautiful; I particularly love to catch Pumpkin Seeds, or Sunnies. They are of a compact shape with a color pattern that would be praised often if they weren't so common: a striking orange belly, orange cheeks with wavy blue streaks, the top half of their bodies greenish with vertical orange or yellowish stripes, blue spots here and there. I have caught some the size of dinner plates, perhaps a pound or more in weight, and they always give a great fight, plunging wildly down into the lake with great force. Sunnies, by the way (more formally called The Common Sunfish, of which there are 38 species) are voracious eaters of mosquitoes. The snobs who thinking fishing for pan fish is only for children are missing out on lots of fun. I often fish for Sunfish with an eight-weight line, much heavier than for trout, so that they won't break the tippet. They are not shy of such thick line, and the stronger line is necessary in case of the odd chance I might hook a pike, a pickerel, or a large small mouth bass. I have found that trolling works, but if I stop paddling thirty feet or so from the lily pads, cast, and play a bit with the fishing line, I have better success.

There are dragonflies and damselflies, hundreds and hundreds of them, especially a species of elegant blue darners, or what we colloquially called darning needles when I was growing up. I suppose that darning needles is a generic term for all sorts of species, but what I've been admiring are actually *supposed* to be termed dancers. I've fished for a couple of hours. Now it's time to watch the dancers. They hover over the water, don't care one bit about my presence. Their speed makes them invulnerable, and that invulnerability makes them quite observable as they don't mind my nearness. They often light on my fly rod. Many of them land on me and my kayak, and they are particularly sexual, mating in midair, on lily pads, on my boat and, again, on me. The males appear to be a more fluorescent blue than the females. The male curls his abdomen over his mate's body where they seem to join behind the female's head, into her back, as it were. She curls her abdomen up to meet his. Strange place to join, I think, but perhaps aliens observing humans might think the same of us.

The Lure Known as the *Mona Lisa*

Richard Brautigan in *Trout Fishing in America* writes about the invention of the world's most perfect lure. Designed by Leonard da Vinci while employed at the South Bend Tackle Company, the lure embodies the perfect fusion between science and art: "He called his bosses in. They looked at the lure and all fainted. Alone, standing over their bodies, he held the lure in his hand and gave it a name. He called it *The Last Supper.* Then he went about waking up his bosses."

How great it would be to have such a fly, a lure utterly failsafe, and how terrible. All the challenge, uncertainty, mystique, and wonder would disappear, as would all the trout, vanishing like the mastodon, saber toothed tiger, giant sloth, and dire wolf. What about a lure that works only sometimes, like all flies? What about a lure called *The Mona Lisa*? What strange shape might it take, having been conceived in the secret stream that wends through the wilderness behind her, the wasteland her odd, coy, vampirish smile invites us to visit? Would the lure be black like her clothing? Would it have blue thread, a color trout can't see? Would it have hair, perhaps a woman's eyebrow hair?

Floaters and Waders

The day had been unusually hot and humid in the North Country, even for August, and, as it was a Saturday, I knew the Battenkill would be thick with a flotilla of canoes, kayaks, and most especially tubes. So I waited until about 6:30 in the evening before venturing out. I parked my truck off a dirt road near a bridge by Camden Creek. I like to wade this winding creek with its banks rich with aster and goldenrod, its pools that sometimes harbor small brookies, amid its chaos and strewn design of deadfall. After a few hundred feet I reach the mouth of the river, a thrilling moment for me because, invariably, reaching a river's mouth from a feeder stream provides the sensation of coming into a vista of light and energy after coursing through a tricky labyrinth.

The floaters are still meandering down the river, but I don't mind. They'll peter out soon. I don't mind when two girls in bikinis float by and smile at me. Next are some boys. Twelve-year-olds, I reckon. One has found a stray beer can in the river and pretending he is guzzling beer (Battenkill-water-brewed) as he floats down. Next a guy and girl (smoking cigarettes) pass in a canoe. He generously tells me there are fish upstream. I thank him, though I already know this. A bunch of young men float by in tubes. They ask how I'm doing and I reply that I've just arrived. One guy asks if I'm going to eat the fish I catch and when I reply that I will release them because I want there to be lots of fish in the future, he looks back at me with disgust. A couple of young women with happy children float by in their canoes, and one of the women exclaims that she has seen lots of fishermen today and all of them were wearing waders. I'm the first she's seen in swimming trunks. I tell her all those guys are a bunch of babies.

Finally, all of the floaters are gone. Dusk is approaching. I love this part of the river for many reasons, one being the multiple currents. The water is warm coming down river, but the current from Camden Creek is delightfully cold. Most of the river in this part of the stream is waist high, with many big rocks for the fish to hide under or near, and the water is clear, so I can see where I'm going. The far side of the river, about twenty five feet away, has evergreens growing right up to its rocky bank, providing lots of shade and food for trout. Upriver is an island completely covered by pink blooming Joe-pye-weed. Down river is a

104

collapsed wooden bridge that makes kind of a dam, and behind that dam is deep, turbulent water. Then the river gets shallow again and, after about five hundred feet, makes deep pools where big trout live. There are guys fishing down river wearing full fly fishing regalia. They appear to be dry flying.

Wearing swimming trunks or cutoffs, sneakers, fly jacket, and baseball cap, I used to get a slight spasm of insecurity, as though I were doing something wrong, but not any more. I try casting upstream, but the current returns my lure immediately. So I cast across stream and down stream. I have tied on a nymph, a #14 Flashback Hare's Ear. No dry flying for me today. Maybe I'm just too lazy to try matching the hatch. Maybe I have little confidence in my ability to do so. Maybe I am just more interested in catching fish the best way I'm able. I soon land, after a fine fight, a 10 inch stocked brown, though the brown looks wild enough, its fins strong and prominent after a few months in a wild environment (newly stocked fish are virtually finless). Then I catch a smaller brown, then a brookie that's not even six inches, a wild fish that makes me feel good that fish are reproducing here.

I know that many fly anglers complain about all the activity on this river. It's one of the reasons I spend so much time fishing in small streams where there are too many obstructions for boats and tubes. Many fishers believe that so much human activity is harming the fishing, affecting trout habits and habitat, which may also be so. But I know there is still good fishing on this river in the morning before people arrive, and in the evening when the floaters head home.

A Bright, Fluvial Flower

While yet alive, before their tints had faded, they glistened like the fairest flowers, the product of primitive rivers; and he could hardly trust his senses, as he stood over them, that these jewels should have swam away in that Aboljacknagesic water for so long, so many dark ages;–these bright fluviatile flowers, seen of Indians only, made beautiful, the Lord only knows why, to swim there!

Ktaadn Trout,   Henry David Thoreau

I let myself sink into the water as silently as possible. It rises just above my crotch, and I wait awhile to adjust to the cool, immobile until comfortable in the water. Stealth is all. I am not of the majority camp that claims casting upstream is superior. Most experts claim that upstream casting is superior because trout face upstream, so if you enter the water behind them, you're less likely to spook them. If one gauges the conditions properly, and is oh-so-quiet, and the stream isn't too low, downstream casting can work just fine, and is more conducive to a meditative type of fishing in which one needn't cast as often. Also, in smaller streams, casting upstream often doesn't work. For example, when there is deadfall in the creek, it is almost impossible to cast over the partially submerged tree, and also foolish, considering the fact that you often want to use a wet fly or nymph and get it under the deadfall where the fish are. When fishing small streams with lots brush and canopy, you want to minimize the number of casts you make. In meadow brooks where there are virtually no obstructions, upstream casting can make sense, but in most cases it just doesn't work when small stream angling. When fishing the small and wild feeder streams of the northeast, upstream casting is often senseless. Frequently the small streams are fast flowing, so they'll simply bring your fly right back to you. When you're trying to make precise casts to avoid over-hanging branches and deadfall, frequent casting is a sure method for catching everything but a trout.

Once acclimated to the water, I peer about 20 feet downstream to a pool at the bend. The bank is webbed with black thorn bushes, and a supernatural white mist hangs over the creek's surface. In less than an hour, the sun will banish this mist, but for now, how I love casting into it, into the unknown where I imagine trout. I don't know how other fly fishers regard the importance of imagination when angling, but for me, it's indispensable. If this were strictly science, then all one would need to do is learn the science and one would catch fish with most every cast. Without imagination, there is no joy in fishing, whatever kind of fishing one does.

I cast and wait awhile. If fish are rising, I can't see them, but I hear a "plop" that sounds like a trout. It's just as much a challenge and experiment in wonder to let fall a Mr. Rapidan beadhead nymph into that liquid unknown. It isn't long before a feisty brook trout, struggling like a demon (though it is I who am the demon), is on my line. I reel her out of the water while moving toward the bank, where I place down my rod to unhook her. She is one of those "bright, fluviatile flowers" as Thoreau described trout, about 10 inches long, and squirming so wildly she unhooks herself and bursts back into the stream.

A Brief Essay on Miracles

Some argue that there are no miracles. Others buy too readily into anything they hear is miraculous. *The Weekly World News* satirizes such people with headlines like, "Hubble Telescope Finds Heaven," "Statues of Elvis Discovered On Mars," "Clintons Adopt Alien Baby," or "Noah's Ark Unearthed in Missouri." Perhaps the miraculous unfolds around us every moment, but it's impossible for us to see. Perhaps our very survival entails *not* seeing the continuous miraculous. After all, if you are tripping constantly you'll probably get hit by a car, drown, or dematerialize into the eighth dimension. I like to think of Christ as a Bodhisattva who performed miracles for those poor souls who couldn't understand they were living in the miraculous each moment. One casts into the stream, and out appears, albeit reluctantly, a miraculous trout. The fact that it doesn't want to leave its element, that one must struggle to witness this alien being, is integral to the sheer delight of it all.

At times when I am fly fishing I'm not sure whether luck or providence guides me. No fish rise, but the stream bends slightly into a deep spring pool where the water is an iridescent green, and I can't see bottom. Surely trout live down there, I imagine. Have I divined rightly? My divining rod will tell me. One of the great pleasures of wet fly and nymph fly fishing is that you can't see the trout rise for your pattern, which is precisely what's fun about dry fly. Instead, with wet or nymph underwater patterns, the clues are subtle, "evanescent and impalpable to the senses," as G. E. M. Skues, the English nymph fly fishing pioneer put it. "[W]hen the bending rod assures him he has divined aright, he feels an ecstasy as though he had performed a miracle each time." When I catch a trout, I feel that ecstasy of having performed a miracle. But there is a responsibility that comes with performing a miracle; the trout must be released. Therefore the exhilaration can be repeated over and over again any number of times you go out with your rod and reel, and with divine luck waiting inside your jacket. All without a bunch of people following you around and bothering you. They'll just have to go out and make their own miracles.

Flies through the Seasons (that I like to use)

Early April: Mr. Rapidan Bead Head Nymphs, Casual Dress Nymphs, #12, Hendricksons

Mid to late April: Royal Coachman, Royal Humpy, #14, Coachman Trude, Blue Quills, Black Caddis Flies, Hendricksons

Late April, Early May: Blue Quill May Flies, Quill Gordon Mayflies, Mr. Rapidan Dry Flies, #12, #14, #16

May: #18 Blue Quill dry flies, March Browns, Quill Gordons, #12 March Brown Nymph, Hendricksons, Red Quills, Light Cahills

June, July.   Spinners and Sulphurs, #16 or 18 Shenk Fox Sulphur dry fly, #12 and #14 Gold-ribbed Hare's Ear, #12 Flashback Hare's Ear, #12, #14, Prince Nymphs

Summer and Fall: Terrestrials. #16 Murray's Flying Beetle. Mr. Rapidan Midges, McMurry Black Ants, #18 Black Fur Ant, #20 Mr. Rapidan Midge. Black Ant and flying beetles, #16-20. Ausable Wulff , Griffin's Gnat, Beadhead Nymphs, Gold-ribbed Hare's Ear.

#10 Woolly Bugger anytime.

Trout Bums

Old Fisherman

Old fisherman spends his night beneath the western cliffs.
At dawn, he boils Hsiang's waters, burns bamboo of Ch'u.
When the mist's burned off, and the sun's come out, he's gone.
The slap of the oars: the mountain waters green.
Turn and look, at heaven's edge, he's moving with the flow.
Above the cliffs the aimless clouds go too.

Liu Tsung-Yuan, 773-819, translated by J. P. Seaton

Fishing lore has many such narratives, and there is no calculating how many of us have gone unrecorded and forgotten, lured away from leading productive lives into living anonymous, useless, creative lives that are near bodies of water. Such fishers are sometimes called Trout Bums, whom I call Zen fishers. I don't know who first coined the name Trout Bum. Surely Trout Bums existed long before the moniker. Possibly the first well-known American trout bum is George Grant, who wrote in *The Master Fly Weaver,* "In retrospect, it now is apparent that I was simply pre-destined to lead an idyllic life wading fabulous western trout streams [and to] enjoy the mystique and the endless variety that is part of the sport called fly-fishing."   Grant called fly fishing "a passport to another world." His greatest quote is an inspiration to all of us who are leading the Zen life of fly angling, or who are simple trout bums: "In 1933 a wonderful thing happened–I lost my job."

All Zen fly fishers are trout bums, but not all trout bums are Zen fly fishers, the difference being that trout bums make no pretensions about spirituality, but care only about fishing, and will do almost whatever necessary to spend a life in the water. The trout bum is a true fishing hedonist, worthy of our admiration, but perhaps obsessed. The trout bum may take up guiding, or may be found in the company of other trout bums, whereas the Zen angler is usually a solitary creature. Such an angler will also make no pretensions to spirituality, but doesn't worry so much about catching fish, big fish in particular. This angler takes in the stream banks, trees, bird life, insects, the brook itself as the fishing experience. Rather than escaping from the world, the fisher has retreated and immersed into it.

Bodies of Water

Terminology regarding bodies of water is often confusing, based more on what locals have named them rather than on any systematic limnology. Warm water fishing takes places in pools, ponds, and lakes, and these designations again are random. Cold water angling is done in streams. In fly fishing lingo, trout are found in streams, a generic noun for rivers, creeks, and brooks. Where I was raised in New England, there were no creeks. Streams that feed into rivers are always called brooks. However, in New York State and Pennsylvania, creeks, or "cricks" are usually the feeder streams that flow into rivers, and brooks are usually small streams that feed into creeks.

A rill is a tiny stream that is too small for fish. Kill is Dutch for river, hence Catskill is Cats River. There is a similar disparity in the naming of lakes and ponds, the naming of which seems more regionally guided than by any rule of size. But anyone who pays attention to language has to eventually acknowledge its imprecision. The imprecision is due in part to local and regional habit. Once something is named, and has been called something for years, there's no motivation to make a change. I remember visiting Walden Pond for the first time, and noting that the pond appeared larger than many lakes I'd seen.

The instability of language itself is also at play. As philosophers like Jacques Derrida have written, words define other words, rather than universally defining the things themselves they are supposed to signify. This isn't much of a problem when they represent objects like tables or doors, but words become less stable in their meanings when describing more abstract concepts like truth or transcendence, which explains the Zen Buddhist's distrust for philosophical understanding. Long before Derrida and his French contemporaries, eastern religions were skeptical of intellectual endeavor as a means of enlightenment. This skepticism is revealed in the Zen koan, which functions to reveal the inherent limitations of language, thereby the absurdity of attempting to apply conventional intellectual understanding to that which cannot be understood through words. By baffling the logical processes of the mind, the koan shows that thought is not the path to spiritual experience, and urges the mind to open up to other forms of understanding. Koans are used to keep thoughts and words from being confused with a reality that is beyond thoughts and words. As Alan Watts says, "Awakening is not to know what reality is...Awakening is to know what reality is not." I think of the Zen masters who devised koans as poets who were not without a sense of humor.

What is the color of space?

Where is the center of the sea?

A Zen master named Gisan asked a young student to bring him a pail of water to cool his bath. The student brought the water and, after cooling the bath, threw on to the ground the little that was left over. "You dunce!" *the master scolded him.* "Why didn't you give the rest of the water to the plants? What right have you to waste even a drop of water in this temple?"

The young student attained Zen in that instant. He changed his name to Tekisui, which means a drop of water.

Zen Flesh, Zen Bones, compiled by Paul Reps

Riding Upon the Wind

According to legend, the writer of the Tao, Lao-tzu, could ride upon the wind, though this is perhaps a poetic way of describing "walking on air," as we might imagine Fred Astaire. To conceptualize a liberated mind is to imagine weightlessness, or at least the sensation of moving through life weightlessly, unencumbered by the grounding weight of desires, wishes, goals, sorrows, anger, fear.

There are probably any number of ways to be free, but they all involve not actually trying to be free. The fisher is trying to catch a fish, but even without catching a fish, what the fisher is doing is challenging and beautiful in itself, in a space that is also challenging and beautiful. The stream is not a fixed place, but a process, a movement, one that the mind can still itself in, and the body is alive inside it.

In Zen *satori* means "enlightened" or "awakened." Professor D.T. Suzuki was often asked what satori is like. His reply: "Just like ordinary everyday experience, except about two inches off the ground!" In part, the point here is that one needn't actually be two inches off the ground to feel two inches off the ground. Personally, I'd rather be two inches off the ground, although such a state might cause distress among my neighbors. And I really have no problem with being two millimeters off the ground, which is the case on good days. How strange that fishing, keeping one's balance in a stream that is slippery and at any moment capable of knocking you off your feet, is such an effective place to practice weightlessness. Your body, busy with the work of maintaining balance, and your mind, focused on the water where you know or imagine fish to be, lose their split. Not only is casting an erasure of the mind-body split, but the entire act of fly fishing can be its elimination, albeit temporary. When a fish is on the line, the fisher is not a mind or a body, but simply a fisher, a joyful, weightless one, as long as she is not thinking, or is letting thoughts evaporate as they come and go, as long as he's not fighting himself, but only that water-rider at the end of the line.

113

Mid-Winter

I am writing this chapter in mid-winter, in the winter's heart, in the part of upstate New York called the North Country. I am in a small room in an old house. It is night. Snow is piled up to the windows, and my three cats are here with me. Leo is asleep on the table in front of me, Cleo drowses under the wood stove where the heat is soft, and Walnut is snoring on my lap. I miss fishing, but right now I love this moment. Most fly fishers are tying flies at times like this. Although I do have plans for flies I'd like to design, nights like these are good times to read fishing stories, or books on fly fishing. I think of the fish, the trout cryogenically stilled beneath the ice floes and ice-glazed streams, where the cold that has slowed everything, including their hearts, penetrates all that it can, and I keep it out of the house as though I were the captain of a small ship, riding out a storm or on a many months' journey through a hostile, frigid ocean, powerful white sea creatures swirling around the house's hulls, its chimneys masts, the souls of the drowned singing in the wind.

The Milky Way, Part II

There may not be more kinds of aquatic insects than stars in the Milky Way, but the numbers can be as daunting. Of the 1,500 species or more that comprise the trout's diet, with thousands of other variations in color and size, some of those variations being infinitesimally different, what vastness of mind could ever seek, let alone manage, to comprise such numbers and detail? No mortal being that we know of. Take heart, however, because the trout don't know any of this stuff, either. To be sure, there is nothing wrong with learning about the thousands of aquatic insects trout feed on, whether those insects are in their subsurface, surface, or flying adult stages.

If you know a dozen or so dry fly species, and can match what is flying around or biting you, you can have the pleasure of fly angling on summer days, rather than locking yourself indoors studying aquatic entomology. The sizes that work best range from #10 to #24 (my preferences are #12, #14, #16). Fly sizes are counter-intuitive to the beginner; the larger the number, the smaller the fly. How so? Hooks smaller than size #1 climb a numerical ladder in even numbers. Hooks bigger than #1 are 2/0, 3/0 and so on. So flies that are #12 have larger hooks than a #14, and the flies themselves get small with the smaller hooks. A #32, fly, for example would be quite tiny, with a hook only about 1/8 inch long (measuring from the shaft's end to where the hook begins its curve).

Effective all purpose fly patterns are Elk hair Caddises (both olive and tan), Blue Winged Olives, Adams, Sulfur, Red (or Blue) Quill Emergers, Hendricksons, and a favorite of mine, the Light Cahill. Favorites of other fly fishers are frequently Woolly Bugger, Gordon Quill, Irresistible, Deer Hair Ant, Trico (spinner and dun), and Spruce Creek.

There are also situations where wet fly and nymphing are more effective. My favorite nymphs are the Lightning Bug, Holy Grail, and The Fly Formerly Known As Prince (Prince Nymphs are quite appealing to trout). My favorite wet fly is the Pheasant Tail. Through experimentation, you may find other flies that are better for you.

A word about the Latin names of the thousands of species of aquatics: It is not necessary to learn them, but reciting them in the right order and combination while in the stream may have the effect of seducing trout to your fly. The following litany has occasionally worked for me:

Ephemerella subvaria, Paraleptophlebia adoptive, Heptagenia elegantula, Cinygmula ramaleyi, Rithrogena impersonate, Epeorus, pleuralis, Siphlonurus quebecensis, Ephemerella infrequens. Repeat this incantation seven times and, if your cast is graceful, there are fish where you are casting, your fly selection is good, and the water temperature is about 60 degrees, you'll catch one.

Screaming Fish

My brother once remarked "If fish could scream, no one would fish."
For the most part, he's right. The only people who would fish would be
the most sadistic. But fish can't scream. Does that mean by virtue of
their silence we can pretend they feel no pain when we catch them? Are
the kindly among us correct who oppose angling as a cruel sport?

Fish do have nerves, but they are not as sensitive to pain as we are.
Ichthyologists are pretty much in agreement, but the verdict on this
matter is still out. Scientists just don't know. Neuroscientists have
argued that a well-developed neo-cortex (as in all mammals) is
necessary for the brain to receive pain signals and that fish, as well as
other creatures that have an "unsophisticated" nervous system, simply
can't feel pain in the way humans and other mammals do, which raises
the question, how have fish survived tens of millions of years without
the necessary capacity to experience, and therefore avoid, pain and
danger?

The answer some scientists offer lies in the concept of nociception, or
the detection of noxious stimuli by the nervous system. The argument is
that fish have the biological makeup to sense and experience noxious
stimuli, like being hooked and reeled out of the water by a two-legged,
hairy fly fisherman, but, lacking a neo-cortex, they just don't experience
the sensation of pain as we do. In short, they don't have the
psychological capacity to experience pain, at least not in the excruciating
way the fisher feels when he accidentally hooks himself. The fact
remains, we just don't really know, nor will we ever really know how or
if a fish experiences pain. This I know: fish have powerful survival
instincts, and do all they can, within their capacity, to avoid being
caught, and whatever it is that fish don't "feel," they surely exhibit what
we'd call fear and panic, and their struggles to avoid being landed are
dramatic and beautiful.

Think of it all this way: If an alien life form that was aquatic had hooked
one of us, and were pulling us into the water, the pain of the hook would
prevent many of us from resisting. However, if we were captured with a
cord around our waist, we'd struggle violently against being pulled
under water. What a fish experiences is fear, which explains its wild
struggle. The sensitivity of our mouths, tongues, lips, teeth, gums and
cheeks lead us to believe that a trout has the same sensitivity, which is

anthropomorphizing the fish. There is no similar tenderness in the jaws of a trout. It is noble to be tender hearted, but kindness shouldn't keep one from the art of fly fishing. Simply release the fish well before it suffocates in the air. Not only does a trout not cry out in pain, neither is it thankful or expressive of its anger, or its gratitude upon release, as mermaids are reputed to be.

I really doubt that being caught is a transcendent experience for fish, even if it's by a dry fly. It's whimsical to think that being transported into the air is the equivalent to the not-so-uncommon human experience of alien abduction or angelic visitation. No, for the fish the experience is probably simply confusing and traumatic. But, without scientific data, I believe the fish forget the experience far more quickly than the fisher.

IMAGINATION, or the Beauties

The beauties of a brook or river
Must be sought,
And the pleasure is
In going in search of them.
Those of a lake
Or of the sea
Come to you of themselves.
(from The Poetry of Dorothy Wordsworth)

I've heard it said that when one scratches beneath the skin of any man, one finds there a six-year-old boy. When I am searching up or down a trout stream for pools or pockets of water that harbor trout, I am indeed as excited as any boy, and like any adventurer in search of a magical, hidden fountain, I am in hopes of finding some secret body of water long forgotten. I scour carefully and deliberately, barely containing my excitement around each bend. In the distance I see where the riffles vanish into a deep pool flanked by thick tangles of poplar or willow saplings, and I have to take care not to slip on the slickened stones.

When I find a stream that feels right, or return to a favorite fishing hole I hold dear, I feel a pervading, electric warmth. When angling in such a place, I am both old and young, ancient and timeless; everything disappears and I am focused solely on fishing. Beneath the surface of every six-year-old boy resides an old man.

Rick Bass in his essay *Why I Hunt* offers as the primary benefit of hunting its stimulation of the imagination. In paying attention to all the details of the landscape or forest, to all the minuscule elements involved in successful tracking, one loses oneself in the activity. To hunt successfully, one must think like the prey, therefore become more like that prey, which requires imagination. One cannot think like a trout, any more than one can think like a deer. But one does get to know their habits, their instincts, their wiles and preferences. I'll see a still stretch of deeper water alongside a shallow current, where there are thick tree roots under water and dark cover made by that same tree and think, a trout might like that place. Or I'll come to an eddy where a brook converges into a creek or larger stream, and think: this is the right place for trout. The water is cool down there. Heron and osprey and other

119

birds of prey can't get at them in that deep water, can't see them or reach them. I'm at an angle where the fish can't see me, so I won't easily spook them. Millions of years of evolution, of natural selection, have refined trout to a skittishness that cannot be ignored if you wish to catch one. Whatever it is about the water that beckons to the little boy in the old man is itself ancient, antediluvian, something the fisher recognizes and emerges into.

Odysseus

A certain type of human requires adventure. Born with a sense of daring and good athletic ability, primarily agility, there are those who need to engage themselves physically. True, the Odysseus of lore didn't seek adventure. It found him. To avoid leaving his homeland and family he feigned madness, then, after a decade of war, and all the boredom, inanity, and horror that entails, all he wanted to do was get back home. Yet he remains the archetypal adventurer. Desire for adventure, particularly in men, is perhaps genetic, and often dangerous. The propensity to war, extreme sports, crappy driving, and drug use all bear this out.

Fly fishing remedies the need for adventure in a healthy manner. I look for streams, or at least parts of streams, no one has fished. I try to get myself into locales most fishers wouldn't consider going into, and the rewards are many. Sure, I get scratched up, bruised, bitten, and scraped, but there is an excitement I feel in getting into places most don't venture, and pursuing fish that know no human artifice.

Thinking like a Fish

The master had become so fond of fishing that over time he left his job in the city to spend all his days in a tiny camp, a fishing hut, not far from the river. Sometimes I would visit him to talk about the world, including, of course, fly fishing. If I brought beer, which helped enliven his speech, I could sometimes gain insights which I might not get otherwise. Once, in an unusually lucid moment, he asked,

"What do fish think?"

"Fish don't think," I answered.

"Do fish not have minds?"

"No," I replied. Then, "Yes, they must."

"Then, if they have no thoughts in their minds, what is in their minds?"

Clearly, the master had given me a koan which might haunt me forever, and I knew that logic would not bring me any sort of solution. In Zen there is nothing to be understood outside of actual experience. The only thing to do was go fishing. Many months later he asked me again about the minds of fish. I could only reply, "Their minds must not be like ours. We are unknowable entities to them. And to think of it, what beings could be odder than fish? Truly they are little aliens."

The master laughed. "The problem with you, Bartow, is you are too clever for your own good. You are evading the question. Remember? What is in their minds? Imagine that fish really do have thoughts and that the thoughts of fish are like the thoughts of the people you meet in dreams." Again, in order to respond properly to the most vexing questions and issues in life, I did the appropriate thing and went fishing.

Some years passed, and now the master, grown quite old, again asked his question. Since the time when he first asked, I had had so much contact with the mute energy of fish that they often appeared in my dreams, no less strange than their existence in the streams where I fished them. An appropriate answer to "What is in the mind of a fish?" might be, "Tonight the constellation Volans will rise in the east and be visible by 10:00 pm." Instead I gave a different answer: "The thoughts of fish are the same as those of the people we meet inside our dreams. What is in their minds is also in the minds of fish. Fish don't think."

The master smiled, offered me another beer.

Red-wings

There seems to be no species of bird more prevalent along the creeks and rivers in the northeast than Red-winged Blackbirds. Maybe you can't always see them, but you sure can hear them complaining while you are wading anywhere near their nests, which seem to be everywhere there is water and wetland. Forget about actually seeing blackbird nests, at least I don't recall having ever seen one. They are well-hidden in reeds and fen stands nearly impossible to reach in marshes only an intrepid biologist would have reason to explore, or along creeks in a tangle of impenetrable brush such as black thorn trees and wild rose bushes.

Seeing Red-winged Blackbirds in March or April has always been a welcome sign of spring for me, but if you pay close attention to these first sightings, they are interesting. The males and females gather in flocks, separately, as though the males are holding a bachelors' convention before the great competition, and the females are conducting their own bachelorettes' symposium. I haven't read ornithologists discussing this behavior, but I am sure they are aware of the trait.

These birds are prevalent throughout North America and love to breed, each pair raising two or three broods per season with three to five eggs per brood. Apparently the males like to mate with other partners, yet while they are doing so, so are their female partners. Clearly they don't mate for life like many other bird species such as swans and cardinals. Perhaps this explains the large flocks that occur in early spring. The partner each bird had the previous summer has vanished into the multitude, and now each bird is preparing for a season with somebody new. Of course this sort of behavior just wouldn't work with humans for any number of reasons, one being that the child rearing period is so lengthy with us, but changing partners is not entirely unknown to us, either.

According to my Audubon Guide, Red-winged Blackbirds sometimes flock in the millions when the breeding season ends. Viewed by some as a health hazard, "Attempts have been made to reduce such flocks by spraying and other methods." Whenever I hear such views, I am disgusted. Why shouldn't there be millions? They are no harm to anyone or anything. The males are a rich black with bright red and sometimes yellow shoulder patches or chevrons. The females are heavily streaked

124

with a dusky brown color. These birds are quite feisty. I often see them chasing off crows that attempt to raid their nests, and they raise quite a fuss while I'm trying to fish. I hear them so often that I've come to ignore them, except when they venture overhead to warn me away. I do eventually leave, but that's because I need to fish elsewhere, and wherever that elsewhere is, there are more Red-winged Blackbirds.

Trouts Remarkable

And you are further to know, that there be certain waters that breed
Trouts *remarkable, both for their number and smalnesse. I know a little*
brook in Kent, that breeds them to a number incredible, and you may
take them twenty or forty in an hour, but none greater than about the
size of a Gudgion.

The Compleat Angler, Izaak Walton

A gudgeon is a small, European fresh-water fish that seldom grows more
than six inches. They are easily caught and used for bait. Therefore a
person easily duped is also a gudgeon, or was so called during
Shakespeare's and Walton's time. Because I fish alone, no one witnesses
my many errors. More times than I can calculate I have caught
submerged branches and my fly has hooked small, pitted stones. One
stone I actually kept because it fought so convincingly. I brought it home
as a trophy, even though it was only the size of a gudgeon, but since
have been unable to find it. Perhaps after all it escaped.

Litter

In the middle of Yeats' poem *The Fisherman* he condemns the rabble, those he considered low-minded, non-idealistic, philistines, whose sense of self worth is based on degrading others and who have no genuine love of beauty. Though I try to fish in remote, small streams, in places most people would think not of fishing in, I inevitably find litter in these haunts. Perhaps I am obsessive-compulsive about litter, but I need to clean it up, to clear it out of my range of vision. I simply cannot adjust to garbage around me, at least when fishing. Somehow the presence of human garbage (redundant–all garbage is human–no other creature creates litter) profanes the place where I fish. Sometimes I remember to bring along a bag or sack for the litter; sometimes I stuff it into my fishing jacket. In general, there are four primary types of garbage that I find along stream banks and in the water: aluminum cans, glass bottles, plastic bottles, and plastic bags. The first three are predictable, but the fourth? I have no idea why I find so many plastic bags caught in branches along banks or half-buried in muck. There are infinitely other human-made objects to be found in streams, but the four I've mentioned are the most common.

For some time now I've pondered what makes someone a litterer. Maybe this isn't a subject worthy of contemplation, but the subject comes to mind every time I find discarded or lost stuff when I'm out fishing. What I've concluded is that there are five primary species of litter bugs. I do not include teenagers here who get drunk and leave their beer cans. Giving them the benefit of the doubt, I assume they might not leave their mess if they were legal or sober, or when they grow up.

Species #1 would be those people whose consciousness has not yet evolved enough to realize that what they do impacts the world around them. Or they do not care that what they do impacts the world around them. Yes, it takes a village to raise a child, but only one slob to mess up the village.

Species #2 consists of those who expect others to pick up for them. They are simply shallow and spoiled. Should we blame the mothers of the world for this condition? Is their behavior caused by mothers picking up after them? Should we not blame mothers and fathers of the world? Unfortunately, every time I collect litter in the stream, I am living up to such spoiled people's expectations.

127

Species #3 are those who have no aesthetic sense. I cannot conceive, nor have any wish to, of people who do not experience beauty. Perhaps such people come to water only to cool off, or for the fun of catching fish, or probably the fun of killing them, or to do other things privately, but I am saddened to think that these places I find breathtaking are just somewhere people casually toss their garbage.

Species #4 are those who believe Mother Nature makes things like cups and soda bottles magically vanish. Actually, these people are correct in principle, but wrong in time scale. Mother Nature is a patient sorceress. How long will she take to make that plastic soda bottle disappear? When archaeologists dig in ancient Greece and Rome, they find pottery fragments that are really pieces of earth. Reassembled as urns, bowls, and pitchers, stories from mythology appear depicted on the pottery, and we are better able to understand the world view, the imaginative and spiritual vision of the ancient Greeks, for example.

Species #5 are the most disturbing. They litter on purpose, not ignorantly or casually, but willfully to do damage out of hatred. Scorn for others, scorn for the world, they view the world (consciously or unconsciously) as a poisoned place and respond in kind. If I had a solution for changing such people, I'd be writing a different book right now.

What will future archaeologists determine about us when, thousands of years from now, they find our Tupperware? Will they conjecture that plastic Barbies are the images of a fertility goddess? Mother Nature will eventually clean up the mess. When the next ice age comes, 10,000 or 20,000 years from now, all our litter will vanish under glaciers. What's the most difficult for me is trying to snatch plastic bags snagged in overhanging deadfall. I worry that I might someday drown attempting to remove these snagged things that are so often over deep and swirling pools. No one would know how I died so absurdly, which would be for the best.

Dead Woodchuck

Like anyone who gardens, I have no love l for woodchucks. (The term woodchuck is an anglicized version of a Cree word, wuchack, which means fisher, weasel, martin.) So when I found one dead on a streambank I felt nothing elegiac. Here lies a bandit, a garden fugitive, I thought, his paws like black rubber gloves, with whitish claws sticking out of them. Staring for awhile, I noticed his teeth were yellow, indicating old age, and figured he perished without someone or something killing him. How many gardens did he raid over the course of his life? I have a grudging admiration for woodchucks; their wily behavior, their rotundity, reminds me of something human. I felt no pity. This woodchuck probably had a pretty good woodchuck life. But something was bothering me.

To witness the dead is to remind of us of life's preciousness, the living energy of the body, for animate life embodied is beautiful, but when the life-force is gone, the remaining body, in its shell form, without its life energy, is as nothing. Normally, I wouldn't think much about finding a dead woodchuck. What disturbed me was that the streambank was profaned with litter. Around this freshly dead form garish plastic and the debris of our careless lives seemed to cheapen all of us.

Catching Giants

A friend of mine who does guiding and boat rentals near the Battenkill State Forest told me that the state had recently stocked two- and three-year-old brown trout in the trophy section of the river not far from his place. (The trophy section of the Battenkill in New York State is regulated as strictly catch-and-release.) Trout that old are big, often more than eighteen inches in length, so I decided to go after some giants, and got myself into the part of the river between two of the bridges where the fish had been released, a section where no one else was fishing. It was a brilliant morning in late May, and I cast beadhead nymphs along the shady side of the river where there were pools near fast running water.

How different hooking big fish in a big river than fishing in small streams! I had a half dozen good fights, and every time a trout took my fly, its tug was powerful, almost violent. The first fish was big; I raised him out of the water before he broke my line, and I realized that if I were to catch fish as large as these, I'd have to play carefully, letting them take some line and tiring them out. Soon after I had another one on. It tore across the water, my fishing line slicing the surface to and fro, all in chaos as I reeled in closer, gave slack, and reeled, slowly gaining on the fish. I had the fish within a few feet of me, writhing in the clear stream. I knew he was too big to lift into the air, but I tried anyway. Of course the trout broke off with my fly, but it was worth the effort to see the fish for an instant shimmering in the air.

Others were biting. Often I could bring the fish in close after several minutes of reeling in, then letting line back out, and wading closer and closer to the hooked trout. Without a net it was impossible to actually land them. They were simply too large to pull out of the water without breaking the tippet line. My small stream techniques were simply not appropriate here. I was able to bring the fish in close, within a couple feet, and could see their stunning gold patterns and black spots shimmering in the water, which was good enough to satisfy me, but to actually lift a fish out the water, I'd have to bring a net to scoop them out. Yes, sometimes you really do need a net.

Stocked trout that are large can be as tough and difficult to land as any wild fish, but I suspect they are easier to catch in that they are less fussy than native or wild trout. (Let's put it this way: I'd rather catch a stocked trout than get skunked). Every nymph pattern I used, from hare's ear nymphs to pheasant tails to beadhead olive caddis, they took. This was great fun, and I am not against stocking as a temporary measure to replace fish while other things are being done, like improving habitat, to replenish wild fish populations. One enormous brown trout, perhaps two feet long, that I played for several minutes and that leapt out of the water before I again lost a fly raising her out above the surface, gave me a thought, one that I'd never get while angling small streams. No matter how great an angler you are, there must always be one stronger than you, too big for you to land. I know there are expert anglers for whom no size is too large, but my belief is that they have simply not yet encountered that great fish. We should all of us, sometime or another, go after a fish that is too big to ever bring in. We should all have the drama of playing a fish we can never land.

Returning for Giants

Next day I returned to the same Trophy Run, this time with my net. I was hungry for more giants. After a while I did snag another, a brown at least 14 inches, and played him back and forth until he was close enough to net, but fumbled around with the net and fly rod, and wished for an assistant to scoop the fish up while I balanced the fly rod. Alas, there was only me. Did I get the trout out of the water? I'm not telling.

I didn't like the extra burden of a net. And in the balmy May weather, there were kayakers and canoeists to avoid, an invasion of privacy I never experience in small streams. Floaters have every right to be on the water, and most are polite. I even enjoy the passing questions sometimes, "Any luck?" and so forth. But I really don't need the company. I hadn't the same luck as the day before. The stocked fish had moved on, or were getting smarter by the hour, but I did catch a little brook trout, a native of the river. When I released him I blessed him as best I could. "Go on, little scupper. Keep away from osprey and heron. Go live in a deep pool where nothing can reach you but things to eat, then sleep there through the winter. Go on and get big and make more of your kind, and perhaps we'll meet again in a year or two." In the meantime, I decided to return to small streams.

Do Fish Have Souls?

Understanding that there are other forms of consciousness in creatures that are not human could be the most important development for human beings in the 21st century. Gauging other embodiments of consciousness in other life forms is not within this book's scope, but let me give an example that relates to the subject. In 1821 the Nantucket whaling ship Essex was stove and sunk in the middle of the Pacific Ocean by a bull sperm whale possibly 100 feet in length and weighing 80 tons. There are differing theories as to what motivated the whale to (intelligently) attack the ship, but mine (and others, such as Nathaniel Philbrick, the author of *In the Heart of the Sea*) is that the whale mistook the ship for a rival male. There was a pod of females nearby, and repairs were beings made to a small whale boat on the ship at the time. The hammering sound may have sounded like a rival bull. If this is the case, then clearly the whale who attacked the Essex was behaving from instinct rather than intelligence.

Soon after returning home from a harrowing ordeal at sea, the first mate of the Essex, Owen Chase, wrote *Narrative of the Wreck of the Whaleship Essex*, in which he described how the whale's aspect had haunted him. Rather than a dumb brute, the whale exhibited intelligence and its behavior was of "decided, calculating mischief." The irony of Chase's quote was lost on Chase himself. It's well known that Chase's narrative was a primary inspiration for *Moby Dick*, but why would an angry, vengeful whale haunt a 19th century whaler so? Doesn't it make sense to those of us in the 21st century who wouldn't be surprised that a whale would defend himself and his kind? But to 19th century whalers, such behavior did not make sense, was, in fact, unfathomable. Why?

To most Americans in the 19th century, the idea that an animal could have emotions, even base emotions such as anger and vengefulness, was incomprehensible, if not terrifying. Terrifying because such an idea makes the vision of a human-centered universe, where only humans were loved (and hated) by a human-like deity who gave his subjects license to plunder nature and kill freely, becomes faulty, if not dramatically unreal. Perhaps what really haunted Chase so was the unspeakable thought that he and his fellow Nantucketers were slaughtering sentient creatures, that his Quaker brethren were destroying beings that were perhaps loved by his God, that possibly even had souls as humans do. Chase never voices this deduction in his narrative, but his turmoil over the whale's behavior seems to beg the question. To acknowledge that a whale might be more than a gigantic, unconscious fish (whalers did not understand that whales were mammals), that a whale might have consciousness or a soul not only spins his livelihood into moral doubt, but his entire world-view. Even Melville concludes in *Moby Dick*, despite carefully examining whale biology and behavior, that whales are fish. The thought that whales might have intelligence or consciousness was unspeakable for Chase and for Melville, perhaps even more unimaginable and disturbing than the danger of cannibalism, which the starving Essex survivors were reduced to practicing upon each other (ironically as a result of their fear to land on nearby islands that might be cannibal).

So, do fish have souls, or do they have a spark of the divine energy we might call soul? Who knows? But if I had to answer the question, I'd say no. Fish are souls, or are all we are able to perceive of a certain kind of soul. Perhaps they are the water's soul, or what little we can know of a much greater being, that little portion of an emanation we only recognize and know as a fish, possibly in a similar, limited way that a trout "sees" the fisher who has landed him. For we can imagine that the trout, when raised out of the stream, sees what we are, whatever it is that we are, in a fully accurate, yet profoundly constricted vision.

Canadian Nightcrawlers

I have learned to read a good trout stream by its litter. In the past, a section of stream with lots of litter was a good place to fish, but is no longer. There is a direct correlation between the presence of litter and presence of fish. People tend to fish where there are fish, so litter could sometimes be a dead giveaway for a decent fishing hole, but those anglers who litter are the same types who kill fish, and keep as many as they catch. I believe I can safely say that fly anglers do not litter. Although probably a small minority, those who use spinner rods and reels are the culprits. Those who use worms also litter. I am not suggesting that all who use worms as bait, and all who fish with the unholy spinner and fishing poles, leave litter. Rather, all fishers who litter are fishers who use spinner reels and worms. Fly fishers don't litter. Those who do vanish mysteriously.

Up and down one of my favorite streams, White Creek, which runs through the village where I live, I find empty white containers. The lids say, in bold brown capital letters, **12 CANADIAN NIGHTCRAWLERS**. The smaller print says **Packed by Weekly's Wholesale Bait Hamburg, NY 14075. Not For Human Consumption.** The price sticker on a recent lid read $5.25. After tax that's about 50 cents per worm. Perhaps the worms are so expensive because they are raised or manufactured in Canada. Perhaps they are Canadian or illegal aliens. I was often incensed when I came across these empty containers, knowing that the sport goes out of fishing when an adult fisher uses worms, and those who use them kill fish. Several of my favorite pools in White Creek where I'd found the containers along the bank or on a sandbar were completely emptied of fish. I considered driving out to Hamburg, contemplating eco-terrorism, but violence just isn't a part of a fly fisher's nature. For a week or two I harbored evil thoughts toward those who used nightcrawlers, trying to will bad karma onto them, all despite the fun I had as a boy hunting them at night with a flashlight after rain. One late afternoon in May after I'd caught (and released) a couple of little brookies in White Creek, and was therefore feeling good having landed fish that day–that's all it takes to make me happy-- I hauled myself out of the water and was standing beside my pickup truck, packing up my tackle. An elderly woman parked not far from me, eyed me suspiciously as I eyed her. She was walking around to the passenger side of her, carrying one of those damned Canadian nightcrawler containers. (I can spot the nefarious objects from a great distance.) When she opened the door, a little boy stepped out, fishing pole in hand.

Perhaps my fly fishing snobbery was taking me to a bad place. After all, I fished with worms into my teens. There is a better solution than practicing the black arts against non-fly fishers. Lots of anglers I know teach fly fishing to children and beginners. That's one solution. Another is to wander. White Creek, for example, is windy and long, beginning in the mountains of Rupert, Vermont, and spilling into Black Creek near East Greenwich, New York. After a few hundred yards Black Creek feeds into the Battenkill. The creek's length is about 20 miles, most of those miles running through a landscape that is rural, undeveloped, or farmland. There are many stretches of White Creek where I find no litter. And that's the trick. Where you can find little or no litter, you'll find fish undisturbed, or visited only by anglers who practice catch-and-release. A fly fisher who catches-and releases leaves no sign, like a Cold Mountain monk. Releasing the trout is part of this practice of tracelessness. The trout can tell us nothing.

Matching the Hatch (or not)

On a cool July morning I was upstream of a sturdy old WPA bridge in Vermont, fishing White Creek, a stream with lots of wild brookies. I was casting in a pool where a current emptied, just before the bridge. Fish were rising there, which always gets me excited. I was using a terrestrial, a #12 Black Ant to be exact, and it worked fine. I landed two brook trout, but it bothered me that the lure I was using wasn't what the fish were rising for. I gazed around to try to figure out what the fish were eating with such abandon. After a little while I could see the hatch, creatures rising from the water on new wings. They were brownish like miniscule ballerinas we see fixed atop music boxes. They rose from the water, spinning, perfectly vertical, and the trout were striking voraciously at these pirouetting fairies that hovered precariously over the stream.

I searched through my box to find what might approximate these flies, but nothing seemed to match them exactly. Two flies did look enough like them to suit me, a blue winged olive, and a tan, elk hair caddis, both #16 (I had nothing smaller) and I was able to land two more fish with them, but still had the feeling that I hadn't quite succeeded. The purpose I had in mind was to fish for wild trout and to catch a couple, which I did. Why anguish over exactly matching the hatch. What works, works. If you're going to agonize over little things like failing to perfectly match the hatch, especially after you've succeeded in getting fish to take your flies, well there's just something foolish going on. Why let obsessive-compulsive behavior ruin your day? Obsession with hatches has to be one of the many paths to madness, especially when critters the trout are rising for are virtually invisible, which frequently occurs. Use your #10 Grasshopper or #12 Black Ant, and don't fret trying to knot on a #24 gnat you can hardly see.

More Dancers

Dancers are everywhere here on this July afternoon at Fourth Lake, in the southern Adirondacks. There are thousands of them hovering and zigzagging over the water, or resting on lily pads, the kayak or me. They are certainly well-named. Flying with precision and abandon just above the water's surface, never colliding, they streak and pause. They dazzle. Their numbers are astonishing. Roughly an inch and a half long with wingspans about three inches, they fly as well backwards as forwards, at lightning speed. They are alert, seldom needing to rest for more than a few seconds. Their four wings are diaphanous and powerful. Dancers, or Short-stalked Damselflies, as my *Audubon Field Guide* calls them, are primarily fluorescent blue, at least that's their dominant coloration on this lake. But many are a luminous green, some a russet brown, some a two-toned green and blue. And, looking closely, the blue varies in shades of purple, gray, and lavender, with occasional black markings. Although there are over 450 species of dragonflies and damselflies in North America (almost 5,000 worldwide), the dominant species here on Fourth Lake seems to be the dancers (one of 20 species found in North America). Because I've seen dancers of different color variations mating, I assume they are of the same species, but exactly which of the 20 species of dancers would require an entomologist to identify. Some species of damselflies can remain submerged in the water for up to half an hour.

These creatures are absolutely fearless, and horny, uninhibited in their sexuality. The male curls the tip of his abdomen (the rear-end section of his body) where his sperm packet is located. When joined, mating in flight or at rest (sometimes on a fly angler in a kayak), the male, having been chosen by the female (according to entomologists), perhaps for his great feats of flight, color, or just plain good looks, hovers over his mate and grasps her by the neck with claspers called cerci. It looks as if the female is being fertilized through the back of her head, but actually she reaches for the male's descending sperm packet by curling the tip her abdomen up to meet it.

The female lays her eggs, one at a time, in or near the water, or in wet wood. The eggs metamorphose into naiads, but not into the mermaids of classical myth. The naiads look nothing like their parents at this intermediate stage of development. They are fierce predators with bristles on the tips of their lower lips that are concealed in their mouths when not in use. They are capable of snaring all sorts of aquatic life, insects, pollywogs (tadpoles), and even small fish or fry. Fully grown, the naiads then morph into flying adults. Adult dancers, by the way, have six long legs, which are, however, unsuitable for walking. They use their legs for clasping surfaces to rest on, or to hold their prey. Their heads are moveable, with huge eyes, and their jaws easily cut into their insect prey. They have absolutely no interest, thank God, in biting humans. They are perfect in what they are.

These dancers on Fourth Lake would have to be considered damselflies rather than dragonflies. The difference, according to my Audubon Guide, is that the damselflies' eyes bulge out the sides of their heads, and damselflies, when at rest, hold their wings to the rear, whereas dragonflies extend their wing horizontally. The dancers (and for that matter all the other species of dragons and damsels) here on Fourth Lake are not simply beautiful and enchanting to observe. These creatures, in both naiad and adult stages, devour huge numbers of mosquitoes, 3,000 per day, the proprietors at nearby Bob's Bait Shop told me, which I later verified.   If all this weren't enough to please, every now and then a fish rises from nowhere attempting to grab one. I suspect they often fail.

Fishing for Smalls

Quite possibly this is the key to fishing: the ability to see glamour in whatever species one may fish for.

Harold Blaisdell

It is early August and I'm fishing for small mouth bass in Arbor Lake, Minnesota, one of the 10,000 lakes. Minnesotans tell me there are more like 100,000 lakes. Of course, any roundish body of water in Minnesota is deemed a lake, some of which are smaller than many ponds I've fished, like the one I'm in right now, which I estimate to be less than 100 acres. As far as I'm concerned, that's plenty big enough to be called a lake.

There are joys to fly fishing in lakes that are much different from stream fishing, the main difference being perspective. Lakes, as Thoreau understood, are more like micro-worlds, or contained universes, whereas a stream is more like a slender body undulating through a world, or the Milky Way cutting across the night's body. I'm in one of those semi-rectangular fishing boats, using a paddle rather than oars, and I'm after small mouth bass. From my boat I count ten houses scattered around the lake, over half of them with docks and motor boats, but it's Monday afternoon and it's just my friend's little boat, the fish, and me. And loons. One suddenly surfaces out of nowhere near me. A mated pair lives here, with their fledgling, which they protect doggedly every time they suspect I'm getting too close to them. Loons are passionately territorial, only one couple per lake, but there are so many lakes that Minnesota has many loons. I can hear their forlorn wails like insane asylum inmates who have wandered to the barred windows to cry into the deaf night, or to wake sleeping ghosts. These birds are amazing swimmers and have the capacity to remain underwater after fish or frogs for a long time. Reports say that loons can dive as deep as 200 feet, but like many lakes in Minnesota, Arbor Lake is shallow, perhaps 12 feet at its deepest.

I could be fishing for perch, or walleye, or pike, those prehistoric monsters, but I'm hooked on small mouth bass. A few moments ago I saw a giant rise up from the lake to snap up a dragonfly, and I've decided to hunt him. My fly rod is behind me as I paddle, trolling for fish. My lure is a Woolly Bugger, which the small mouths seem to like just fine. My uneven paddling, I guess, is making the bugger simulate a naturally moving streamer. The challenge is when my reel sings wildly with a fish on, I have to stow my paddle, lift the rod, and then land the fish. Sometimes I lose one, sometimes I land one, but the beauty is the fish's behavior. Small mouths rise out of the water like rainbow trout. I love to see them breach the surface as though they're trying to take flight. Naturally, I never do get that big one.

Muskrats

Only those who become weary of angling bring to it but the idea of catching fish.

Raphael Sabatini

Sometimes while fishing you see things that you just wouldn't if you weren't out on the water fishing, doing about as close to nothing as you can, like the time I saw an osprey land on a dead tree bough. The osprey was so big the branch couldn't hold her weight, and came crashing down into the river. Naturally I took the osprey to be a good sign that there were fish in the deep pool she'd landed over, but possibly she took me to be a good sign that there were fish there. The osprey flew off immediately after the racket she caused, most likely because the disturbance probably frightened every fish for miles up and down stream. I can't begin to calculate the many times I've seen kingfishers, blue herons, and green herons, and in May all sorts of yellow warblers I would never have seen if I weren't in a stream.

Once I thought my eyes were playing tricks as I watched a leafy branch moving across stream rather than downstream. It moved deliberately, as though possessed, until eventually I saw the branch reach the opposite bank and realized it was being guided by a muskrat. I have often seen muskrat burrows that lead to their dens along creek banks, but they often build houses or lodges, as high as five feet in marshes, out of vegetation such as cattails. Because their chief food source is vegetation, I don't know if the muskrat I saw that day was gathering food or building material. Muskrats will also eat mussels, frogs, crayfish, and small fish. Apparently muskrats are quite prolific. I see lots of them while fishing, and have since learned that they can have as many as five litters per year with as many as 11 per litter.

I like muskrats. There is something joyful about the way they live and swim, cruising beneath the surface like seals. They can remain underwater for long periods, and seem to swim as well backward as forward with their flat rudder tails and webbed back feet. I was somewhat disturbed, though I hid it, when talking to a young guy who traps them for fur. Obviously their fur is waterproof, which must make it valuable, but one would have to trap lots of them (close to 10 million were trapped in the 1980's). The fellow who traps them gave me a number he trapped last year; I think it was over 100, but I don't think he gets much money for each pelt. He just likes trapping, something I don't understand. The practice seems downright cruel, especially against these creatures that are both harmless and playful. As I said, the common muskrat is prolific, and I do see lots of them, which consoles me.

Something he said about muskrats has stuck with me. He claimed they were stupid, that when the trap springs they will dive into the water, thus drowning due to the iron trap's weight. (According to guidebooks I've checked, muskrats can remain underwater for as long as 17 minutes before surfacing again for only a few seconds.) I've thought about his comment about their so-called stupidity and don't believe such behavior signifies lack of intelligence. I'm not going to argue that muskrats are actually intelligent; I just don't believe his example has any significance in such a test. If an alien being were trying to trap you, and you were in intense pain and nearly paralyzed by fear, reason wouldn't function, only instinct, and your instinct would drive you most likely to flee into your most familiar element. For the muskrat, of course, that's water. Muskrats are mammals that appear to enjoy themselves at all times, and seem completely and intensely engaged in whatever they are doing.

Clearly, because I eat meat and like fish, yet am open to recognizing consciousness in others, I've had to come to terms with causing pain, and have discussed already that fish probably don't experience physical pain, solely instinctive fear, fight, and panic. I am not bothered much by this because I am convinced of the dimness of consciousness in fish, unlike muskrats which, in the spectrum of consciousness in nature, exhibit intelligence and emotion.

Memory and Fish

Trout do not have memory. At least, it's highly doubtful that they do. I think their version of memory is genetic, tens of millions of years of inherited instinct, successful tendencies of behavior that are spontaneous, passed on over eons, manifested in the fish we see rising in the distant pool for that hatch or caterpillar that has dropped from a branch. A trout probably doesn't think about going after that caterpillar any more than we think about taking a breath or willing our heart to beat.

I believe that fish live strictly in the present. Given this aspect of fish "consciousness," the fishes' experience of the present has important consequences for anglers, and for all those others who might seek illumination, that thrill one occasionally gets from a "true" apprehension of the present, a brief beauty into which we ourselves disappear. For this is known: we are not fish. We do not truly wish to lose ourselves, for the ego consciousness to vanish over any extended moment. Think: would you really wish to lose your memory? Would you truly want to lose the ability to project into the future? (If I try to swim from Long Island Sound to Spain I will drown. If I cross the street while that trailer tractor truck is coming, I will be crushed.) We cannot survive without the faculty of reason, and we would not be human without it. Without this long evolved gift of reason, memory, and imagination, what would we feel beyond instinctive impulses? These gifts are also conditions of beauty. We are learning more and more that intellect, faculties of reason, of memory, do not belong strictly to humans, but are present in apes and monkeys, and in fishy beings like dolphins, otters, whales, and seals, but reasoning is not present in fish.

The evolution of reason is a grand thing, and need not necessarily lead to the disparagement of intuition. We need reason, as we need ego. We need memory and intuition (which in humanity is refined instinct). And we need the means to become lost in moments or Wordsworthian "spots of time." We need it all. We most especially need to catch a fish now and then.

In the streams and inside books I've heard and read fly anglers frequently say things like, "that trout remembers being caught on that fly," or "those trout have seen this fly too many times. I can't fool them any more with it." How can that be? The only reasonable answer is, it cannot be. Whatever the myriad reasons the trout may not be taking the lure, its refusal most likely has nothing to do with anything approximating memory. Maybe the trout can "see" you. Maybe the trout's just not that hungry, or no longer hungry. Maybe the lure you're using doesn't look enticing. Maybe the fly looks weird because of the way it's twitching (or not twitching) in the water—you're committing the sin of drag. Maybe the fish just doesn't like the way you're dressed, or you exude an aura repellant to her.

If given the fact that fish do live in an endless present, then this condition has implications for those of us who fly fish. For example, the near-universally held belief in diminishing returns when casting, that is, with each failed cast our chances of landing those trout we see rising in a pool thirty feet away is decreased, may be false. I realize that I am disputing the experiences of many fishers, and have often myself felt a strong sense that I have exhausted or played out a particular fishing hole or pool. Fish will simply not bite or rise endlessly.

Yet, the fish are not going to recall your poorly chosen lure, sloppy cast, or the drag that makes your pattern seem unnatural or threatening. Try again. Cast again, change your fly. Trout don't remember. Nor do bass. Nor do any of the other fish people. Time and time again experience has proven to me that by changing my lure I've been able to get a fish to bite. Sometimes many changes have been necessary. So simply stand there in the water and pretend you are doing a science experiment. Actually, you don't have to pretend. Enjoy the fact you are outdoors in the center of a stream on a blue planet in the Milky Way's stream somewhere in the universe, in the center of the universe. Actually, according to contemporary astro-physicists, all places in the universe are at its center. Revel in this fact.

I cannot guarantee changing your lure will work. There are too many variables to make a guarantee. But switching flies has often worked for me. Changing the fly's movement in the water is also a good idea. Many, many times I've got trout to bite simply be stripping out more line and letting the current take the lure away, creating a natural motion.

Shopping Cart Graveyard

I am in Furnace Brook, a small stream that I have mistaken for Harold F. Blaisdell's local fishing haunt, and inspiration for many of his speculations in *The Philosophical Fisherman.* This is another Furnace Brook, in Bennington, not Pittsford, not the pristine stream of Blaisdell's, though surely this Furnace was once a stunning trout stream. It's windy, with surprising twists and turns, with pools and small islands here and there. Its banks remain stable and the water is crystal clear, despite the fact that it had been raining for days. Litter is everywhere: the usual beer and soda cans, plastic bags, old diapers, and enough tires to make a treacherous obstacle course. It would take an army of volunteers to clean the debris here, so I don't bother to pick anything up. The futility of cleaning this pretty little stream is too much. My choice is to fish, or to dedicate the next month or so to cleaning this mess. I choose to fish.

There are ruined shopping carts everywhere up and down the brook. If managers at the local supermarket have wondered where their carts have disappeared to, I've solved the mystery. Perhaps the homeless have slummed here in the past, or possible the carts have been dumped here from the apartment complex that borders the stream. There's a good barrier of brush, trees, a strong metal fence between the complex and this section of Furnace Brook. The Furnace is small, much of it too small to fish but for this section that leads into populated Bennington. The shopping carts are scattered along banks and half sunken in the brook like the remains of weird little shipwrecks. I wondered if there could still be trout in this old Furnace?

Despite the ruins, despite the mess, I love this brook. You may recall Dr. Seuss's 1947 book, *McElligot's Pool*. The book begins with the boy Marco daydreaming by a tiny, polluted pool, fishing pole in hand, nervous worm dangling furtively in the water. There is debris, an old shoe, clock, tin cans and bottles in McElligot's Pool, and later in the book in the distant background a factory spewing smoke into the summer sky. Yet Marco is undaunted. He fishes where he is, imagines the pool snaking beneath his polluted town, reaching the ocean where marvelous fish dwell. Dr. Seuss's boy-hero is able to see the pool imaginatively, through the ruin around him, as though it were merely a temporary obstruction, and envision the underlying beauty and magic of, not only his pool, but the uglified world around him.

146

The story clearly has an early environmental subplot, and it's no coincidence that the pool has a Celtic name. The Irish are known for their ability to imagine beauty and wonder in the face of squalor, the pool being a place which through whimsy and love might be transformed. The Scots are known for inventing modern fly angling. The hero of the story is Quixotic. But, after all, idealistic hope makes possible imaginative transformation, and is always, though risking absurdity (it takes courage to risk being absurd), better than cynical realism or hopeless fatalism. We might keep in mind that the great irony of Cervantes' *Don Quixote* is that the title character (in his fictional context) really is a noble knight errant, truly is courageous and chivalric in a world where no other knights exist, have never existed, except as poetical inventions.

Most of fly fishing does not involve casting and casting, at least not in the way I like to fish. It involves watching, seeing through things, being carefully attentive to the stream you are in. Having walked well upstream, through the strange graveyard where shopping carts go to die, I am moving carefully downstream. Are there fish here? The brook twists into a bend, near an island of reeds and Joe-pye-weed. Just beyond the miniature island is a pool deep enough to appeal to trout. At the front of the pool rises the cage of a shopping cart, and at the pool's edge is another cart in the water, tipped on its side, casually rusting. I'll have to cast accurately between the carts if I am to avoid catching them instead of a fish. I tie on a Griffin's Gnat, #16, and, after a couple of false casts with my trusty little one ounce, land my fly into the pool. In moments I land a fine little brookie, then another, and another, two of them wriggling violently off the hook before I have to release them myself. But not before I get a good look at these haloed creatures that only the wildest of imaginations could create.

Extra Terrestrials

When I began fly fishing I didn't care too much whether or not I caught a trout. Sure, I wanted to catch fish, but I knew that fly fishing was difficult, so I just decided to enjoy the water, the clouds, the birds. Standing in a river with a fly rod in hand gave me something to do while standing in the river on a hot afternoon. But when I learned to locate fish, I became more and more determined, if not obsessed, to land one, and would spend hours at a pool, testing different fly patterns until I could get a trout to hit my cast. That's how I discovered terrestrials. Well, sort of.

One afternoon my sweetheart came out fishing with me, not to fish, but perhaps to observe my other passion. We went to White Creek, to an area where I knew there'd be wild brookies. I wanted to show off a bit, but even more, I wanted her to see a trout, to witness the beauty of these fleet creatures. But nothing was working. I couldn't get them to take dry flies or nymphs. There was a Black Ant lure in my fly box that I must have bought with a set of other flies. It had always, like other terrestrials, looked like an unpromising lure to me, but sure enough, shortly after casting into a rippling pool I caught an eight or nine inch brook trout. Thus began my love affair with terrestrials.

What exactly are terrestrials as opposed to dry flies or nymphs? Terrestrials are patterns that simply mimic non-aquatic insects, such as ants, grasshoppers, crickets and beetles. Terrestrials comprise the lures fly anglers use that are often effective in most any situation. Terrestrials work like dry flies in that they float on the water, but you can twitch your fishing line a bit to make it appear as though struggling on the surface, as though they've accidentally fallen into the stream. They are highly effective during high summer and through the autumn, when ants, crickets, beetles, and other insects abound. I like terrestrials so much that I always keep many extra terrestrials in my fly box.

Rain

The previous couple of days fishing had left me blue. I'd gone fishing in places where I'd previously caught trout, fine deep pools with lots of cover and room for casting, but the fish were gone. Telltale signs were present: Beer cans, lots of them, and empty earthworm containers. The fish killers had emptied the pools. I collected the cans, enough to pay for a bottle of good India Pale Ale, which helped me weather the pisceacide, and resolved to return to fishing in those places that are just too much trouble for most other anglers, especially those worm fishers and pesky little boys, to reach.   .

I started early, took my fly rod, parked my pickup truck behind a church (no one ever bothers you for parking in a church parking lot) and rode my bicycle a couple of miles to the bridge where I entered the creek, then wandered about a half mile upstream where I'd fish my way back down. There were lots of small, but catchable brook trout in the pools and pocket water of White Creek, but nothing was rising. The fish even ignored my #14 Black Ant, my favorite terrestrial, my sometimes go-to fly when nothing else works (my other go-to flies when nothing else works are the Gold-ribbed Hare's Ear, The Flashback Hare's Ear, the Woolly Bugger, and Griffin's Gnat). Then, up ahead, I saw rainfall peppering the stream as the storm moved toward me. There was no lightning, no thunder. I get out of the water when there's lightning. I like to think that I'm not a complete dunce. But the rain poured down. It was midsummer, and I wouldn't have minded much because I was wearing the usual: swimming trunks, T-shirt, sneakers, but I'd forgotten my baseball cap in the truck. The bill of the cap would have made life much easier, would have enabled me to see in front of me. I tried casting in this deluge, but it was just ridiculous in the storm. I got drenched. Suddenly all seemed rather absurd, humorous. I suppose once you're completed soaked, you return to some childhood memory, or perhaps because you're all wet, you no longer have to worry any longer about getting all wet. I felt strangely elated as I began my long trek back down stream to my bike and then to my truck. I never made it, at least, not until much later.

The rain vanished almost as quickly as it appeared. I turned back and went back to the one pool where I'd seen a fish rise. I knotted on my Black Ant. I cast into the pool. I caught a trout. This scenario repeated itself several times over. Why was I suddenly catching fish that I couldn't even get to nibble before? I don't know, but here are my guesses. Because I was casting downstream, it was harder for the fish to see me after the rain. Perhaps the rainfall drives more edible creatures into the water, which stirs the fishes' appetite. Perhaps fish get more aggressive when the water is a little cloudy. Also, the stronger currents generated by the rain makes the fly appear more natural as it drifts faster through the water. Fish can't reason. They act on instinct, impulse. If they could think, they might conclude that no one would be foolish enough to get caught in such a storm, thereby deducing that it's safe to bite just after the rain. I was as wet as every one of the fish I landed and released. Happily, as the sun flared through the clouds, I felt a surge of largesse toward all fish and fishers. May all adult worm fishers who litter take the long way to heaven, which entails spending one long and humid summer afternoon in hell.

No Zen

High, high from the summit of the peak,
Whatever way I look, no limit in sight!
No one knows I am sitting here alone.
A solitary moon shines in the cold spring.
Here in the spring–this is not the moon.
The moon is where it always is–in the sky above.
And though I sing this one little song,
In the song there is no Zen.

                    HAN-SHAN (trans. Kenneth Rexroth)

It's difficult to say why certain streams in the northeast are called rivers, creeks, or brooks. The Indian River is certainly long enough to be a river, about 10 or twenty miles, but it winds like a maze and is narrow and shallow enough in places to be a backyard brook, with brush so thick along the banks you'd never know a river was there, but for its gurgling voice. The Indian is wild with deadfall around every bend, spring pools, narrow currents along curving banks, occasional islands with head-high ferns. The river is not always benign, which is partly why I'm attracted to it. Once I witnessed a copperhead in the process of swallowing a fingerling trout. The banks are rife with stinging nettle. The grapevines can be so thick you'd swear they are actually trying to trip you.

Two days before I'd blundered into the river, splashing, making too much of a ruckus in a section I'd never fished before. Immediately I saw black, ghost-like shapes scatter in the water, which made me over-anxious. Those little black ghosts were up and down the river, but my excitement made me oafish. Hurrying seldom pays off when angling. A good fisher needs to be stealthy, if not graceful. Every spring pool I approached seemed to have fish, but I kept scaring them by moving too abruptly, failing to sneak up on them, or by quitting each pool too soon. There were always fish behind the small islands made by clumps of grass and rocks in the river, but these too I quit too soon, only to see trout dart away as I approached. Horse flies were also tormenting me (I'd forgotten to put repellant in my jacket). I had carelessly scratched my legs on raspberry vines, brushed stinging nettle against my hand (each leaf must carry a thousand infinitesimal spines) and I kept snagging my fly and line in overhanging branches or tall grass. One problem was that the tippet line I was using was too long for fishing in such close quarters. I was nymphing, using a scud nymph, a lightning bug, and the Fly Formerly Known As Prince--always good lures for nymphing, but the trout would nibble or tug once or twice, then quit. Eventually I lost all three flies in stream snags or in the canopy. But I stubbornly kept to the nymphs. After several hours, I climbed back up onto the old railway track, now a hiking trail, and returned to my truck. I was skunked.

I returned to the Indian River two days after my dismal failure to catch any fish. Simply put, I had fished poorly. When I returned I knew what I was up against, which was primarily myself. This time I came wearing old blue-jeans (I would've ripped waders to shreds on the thorn bushes), a short tippet line, under seven feet, and insect repellant. Immediately I saw fish rising in a spring pool which the stream's current cut across.

Again I tried a scud, then an iko caddis, but after a tug on each, the fish lost interest. Because the fish were actively rising, I decided to try dry flies. I knotted on a little blue wing olive, and let the current drift the olive into the pool. Within seconds (okay, in under a minute), one of those little black ghosts took my fly. Lo, it was no longer a shadowy thing, but a trout with a silvery back and a pinkish rainbow along his sides. I am always astonished how different the fish look when you hoist them out of the water, how magically they transform in the light, as though they are one type of being while in the water, and change into another creature as you are reeling them out. The trout was so feisty he flipped himself off the lure as I admired him, saving me the trouble of having to unhook and release him. Over the next several minutes (if they were minutes, for time seems to alter itself when the fishing captivates) I caught two more wild rainbows.

Among the obvious lessons from the Indian River experience is the importance of changing strategy. You need to experiment with flies. When you see fish rising, you should experiment with different lures until you hit on one the fish will take. In my case, I had been fixated on using nymphs, whereas dry fly lures turned out to be a better choice. No two situations are ever exactly alike. You needn't try hundreds or even dozens of dry flies. A few good varieties will usually work, such as blue winged olives, elk hair caddises, red quill emergers, sulfurs, spinners, blue quills, parachutes, or light cahills. I've had great luck with bigger,

152

finicky, wild browns with numbers 14 and 16 yellow and orange stimulators. Though not a sex toy, the yellow and orange stimulator looks gaudy as an Io moth.

Perseverance is a virtue, but stubbornness is not. Ralph Waldo Emerson tells us, "A foolish consistency is the hobgoblin of little minds." Trying different flies is simply good sense.

Thoreau, Tom Bombadill, and the Connemara Man

The Fisherman
Although I can see him still,
The freckled man who goes
To a grey place on a hill
In grey Connemara clothes
At dawn to cast his flies,
It's long since I began
To call up to the eyes
This wise and simple man.

W. B. Yeats

Fly fishing ruins your life in a beautiful way. Many of the things that were important to you get forgotten, so that only the most pressing concerns can be given attention. The lawn grows taller, the garden turns to wilderness, the paint flakes off the house, you're missing those meetings you never really wanted to attend. Instead you're in a creek; it's high summer, the hills shimmer blue in the distance which you can barely make out through the witchery of angles the black thorn trees make. Your head is barely visible above the stream bank, and those in passing cars on the near road couldn't catch a glimpse of you if they tried. Oh, and by the way, there are wild trout in this neglected stream. This practice of disappearing from the world of humans is something you get better at the more you try.

Is our purpose here on earth to discover joy? The world is a horror show, with human beings doing inhuman things to other beings daily and on a mass scale, joyless humans spreading their joylessness. Yeats' Connemara Man is above, literally and figuratively, the world's strife and human ugliness. He is a devoted fly fisher. His existence is saintly, unsanctimonious, grounded in the elemental life like a Cold Mountain poet. His life is one of mythic invisibility.

J. R. R. Tolkien's Tom Bombadill is a pure man, in love with the natural world, in love with his consort Goldberry, in harmony with all creation, completely immune to the dark powers, and completely unengaged with the war surrounding him and threatening to engulf Middle Earth. Who would want Bombadill or the Connemara fisherman to be any different? They stand as emblems for our better selves. Then there is Henry David Thoreau. Like Bombadill and Yeats' angler, he too is mythic. Yet Thoreau was not an imaginative creation.

Once, in my early twenties, I read an essay on Thoreau's conundrum: whether to live divorced from obligations to his fellow humans, which Thoreau seems to have been capable of, or to take up active political engagement against evil. Surely he found the genocide against indigenous Americans repulsive. We know he was passionately abolitionist, and was against the Mexican War, which he considered expansionist and immoral. Yet we know Thoreau's preference was to spend time in the woods, hiking, canoeing lakes and rivers. I am not familiar with any writings by Thoreau in which he expressed angst over these two conflicting forces of attraction, yet I cannot help but feel that this book would be lacking if it did not address the problem.

I don't know the answer. "The Answer" as a simple, single formula, does not exist. I do not trust do-gooders who condescend to those who've found happiness in a simple life, who are not engaged in "fixing" the world. And I recall in grad school in the early 1990's those effete fools who behaved as though maintaining the correct literary theories were adequate engagement with the world, people who'd never dream of devoting a day at a soup kitchen or joining an environmental group.

As I write these words I cannot deny the dread I feel about the impending environmental crises that looms before us in the not too distant time ahead. Doom caused by climate change is not science fiction fantasy, and the idyllic picture of angling I have been painting in this book will vanish as though it were a fiction. It will be one of the less significant things that we will lose. The science deniers, whether motivated by ignorance or greed, must not prevail. What would Tom Bombadill do in our situation? He had magical powers. Most of us who are aware of the impending danger have only the world we cherish and our ability to communicate the facts of a possible catastrophe. Poet Carl Dennis is his *Practical Gods* writes, concerning Jonah, *a prophet's supposed to redeem the future, Not predict it.* Scientists and environmentalists are not prophets, but are presenting us with facts. Maybe the small fact of this book about the small world of fishing in little streams might contribute an infinitesimal part of a grander vision that will lead us from the mad path we are on.

155

At the same time, I have no problem with the world's Connemara men and women, though I have to confess, they are few and far between. Frankly, there are not enough of them, not enough of us who take complete joy in what we do and how we live, which are the same thing. I'd argue the world needs more Bombadills as examples of the lives of beauty I like to think we are all, in some way, meant to live. And I like to think those truly noble souls who've dedicated their lives to environmentalism or ending human suffering are following their bliss, as Joseph Campbell would put it. Surely there are not enough of them, or us, either. So we can look to Thoreau for an answer to the question: to goof off fly fishing or to save the world? Whatever your work is, if you are not deriving joy from it, then something cannot be right. By simply following those things which interested him, and which he loved doing, which certainly included what many called goofing off, Thoreau possibly had more impact on the world than any number of unhappy crusaders and do-gooders.

Many of us fall somewhere in the middle as, in a sense, Thoreau did. Like fly fishing, life is a balancing act. But for my part, let there be more like the Connemara fisher, as Yeats described, *A man who does not exist,/ A man who is but a dream.*

Cows

Early evening, late August, I parked by truck on a dirt road just off highway 30 in Vermont, got my fishing gear ready and stepped gingerly into the Mettowee River. I moved quietly under a bridge, listened to the cars echoing overhead as I prepared my tackle, ducked beneath the spider webs, each with a large brown-speckled sister at its center, then emerged back into the light and looked for the cows in the bordering field. They weren't nearby. Good. The first time I'd fished here about a dozen of them came to greet me, perhaps out of curiosity, perhaps looking for food. Possibly I reminded them of the farmer who cared for them. I was surprised by their interest in me, and a little annoyed that they were *amazing* the fish.

In the pool a bit down river from the pasture, I began to cast where I knew lots of fish live because of the good current, and the large stones they could hide under. Nothing. After trying a couple different flies, something large stirred overhead, and a falcon suddenly launched, circled around me, vanished. Perhaps the falcon's presence scared the trout, so I decided to tread farther down-river, to another pool under a leaning sycamore. The sun was setting, the banks were rich with golden rod, milkweed, jewelweed, asters, gaudy with yellow, orange, pink and mauve. Monarch butterflies were abundant, and their random flights cast shadows over the stream. I could still hear cars and trucks from the highway, but they were far enough away to sound soft. From the barns and silo nearby scores of swallows darted overhead and lined the telephone wires.

With a hare's ear pattern I caught a brilliant rainbow who came leaping immediately out of the water, and I didn't see her again until landing her. I hooked another that also leapt from the stream straight away, but this one got away before I could get him in. That was okay. I was calm, happy with my fishing, ready to walk slowly back to my truck. The cows were waiting for me. We stared at one another. There was something about their eyes that gave me pause, eyes large, dark and warm, curious. Calm, gentle. Possible a touch of sorrow, but I believe contentment. No bulls around. Sort of a shame, but better for me at the time. (As a child, I loved to stare out the car as we passed farms and pick out the bull.) It dawned on me that cows as sweet as these must be tended by a kindly

157

farmer, or his children, whose warmth must have been transmitted to the cows. The barn in the distance looked run-down, but the house appeared in good shape, a straight frame colonial.

These were Holsteins, with their random black and white patterns. The cows had a yellow tag attached to each of their enormous, troll-like ears. The tags made the cows appear as though they were wearing earrings. On the left ear was a number, on the right, a name: Bat, Bette, Lulu, Olive Oil, Silva, Dusty, Cindy, Faun, Ella, Glory, Mel, Violet, Flack, Birdie, Libby, Marli, Lacey, Ktyna.

Terrestrials, Part II

Perhaps the arcana of fly angling is difficult because of the complex entomology of insect stages, so bizarre compared to human development. We begin, like aquatic insects, in the water, but we don't hatch into nymphs swimming freely in a watery womb where other creatures live and want to eat us. We don't turn into emergers, with brief, new bodies, floating to the stream's surface, where our metamorphosis continues, and we don't radically transform, again, if a fish doesn't scarf us down, into winged creatures who fly away (again if lucky to avoid being fish food) to mate. No, we begin as aquatic beings, but after we are born our lives on earth are strictly terrestrial. We may dive in submarines or fly in jets, but only if terrestrial conditions are artificially reproduced.

As challenging and fun as it can be to match the hatch, sometimes there is no hatch going on to match. Terrestrials, those insects not born from the water, will often make a fish rise when nothing else will. They are particularly effective when cast near stream banks and in water that may not be quickly moving, under trees, so when cast they can be made to appear as though they've fallen into the water from on high.

Maybe it's not strange to use lures that imitate something real to catch a fish. What is strange is using imitations that resemble nothing in the natural world that we know of. What is fishing, after all, but a form of connection, ultimately connection with fish and, often, with the unexpected. Are there not two great questions we ask in this life, one of which is "Why are we here?" One answer is that life is its own answer. Another, to witness. Another, to connect. But the word "connect" is such a tepid, insipid word. Perhaps that which we call soul is energy, the connection between inner and outer. In Zen inner and outer are mental constructs that, ultimately, do not exist. Maybe we are split from unity at birth so that we may ultimately connect with the stars, whence we've come. While doing so, or not, I'm trying to *connect* fish to a wiggling terrestrial.

Birch Pond

I discovered the enigma that is Birch Pond by accident, or by design that feels like accident. The pond, though it seems a most unlikely body, presents a fine place to fly fish. Birch is a kettle pond, formed in the last ice age, about 12,000 years ago, when a glacier scraped through and left a block of ice that became a pond with a soft sandy bottom. It's also a genuine pond in terms of size, certainly less than an acre, less than half a dozen Olympic swimming pools combined into an oval. The pond lies in a small valley, about two-thirds of the water surrounded by forest, the remainder flanked by a path through a small meadow. Off a steep bank is a rickety dock missing boards that reaches about six feet into the pond.

I decided to try fishing Birch Pond on a whim. It's located in a conservation forest and farm, and I often hiked past it in winter wondering if any fish lived inside. On a cloudy June afternoon I decided to try it out, hiked the difficult two or three miles, figuring there might be lots of pan fish, even some small bass. As my little mutt Lola and I came around the bend, we scared a blue heron off the water. As it ascended in its lumbering, ungainly flight, I thought, "Fish." There was also a little green heron that took flight, and a flock of cedar waxwings hovering over the pond. I've seen waxwings before, feeding off a hatch together with trout. Suddenly a large trout spilled out of the water, then another, and another. The little pond was teeming with trout.

How was it this pond had so many wild trout? Trout are cold water fish. This was a warm water pond, or so I thought. I'd fished in this forest before, catching little brookies in its pure, tiny streams. No brooks in the forest large enough to maintain large trout, the answer to this mystery is that at least one good cold stream runs steadily into the pond's far side, where the woods are marshy. Twenty or thirty feet from the dock, opposite the marsh, is a culvert where the water runs out of the pond in a torrent to a steep and stony stream. Thus there's a strong cold water stream-flow through the pond. In essence, the pond functions like a giant spring pool one might find in a big trout river. The discovery left me ecstatic. Virtually no one fishes this pond.

I didn't do so well my first time in Birch Pond. Lola was out on the dock with me, and a couple times I forgot about her and tripped into her. I was also worried about accidentally hooking her, but I didn't want to leave her home. She's half King Charles Spaniel and half miniature Doberman, a high energy dog who loves hiking with me, so the next day I brought a hammer and stake and leashed her far enough away to watch me in safety. The stake in the soft bank would come in handy, as I knew I'd be returning again and again to play the difficult trout. Certainly I'd forgotten about Zen. I was at Birch to catch trout, and returned again and again for the same goal. I do not know Zen. No one "knows" Zen. The basic premise of Zen is that Zen must be experienced. One cannot understand Zen in the way one understands Plato or calculus. Fly angling is a practice. Like other practices that involve silence, intuition, calm, there is a certain "not doing" that is necessary. Fishing at Birch completely possessed me. Just me and the pond and the fish with Lola resting behind. But what I was not doing was catching fish. The hell with Zen.

Birch Again

Kettle ponds have crystalline water, and Birch is no exception. The water is translucent green, its intensity varying with the sunlight. The shifting colors can be mesmerizing. Even more mesmerizing is looking into the water, rather than at it. Looking down into the pond is like looking at a forest from your window on an airliner. Or better yet, because the pond is never really still, like looking into a crystal ball and seeing a forest under water. The trout love the straight green weeds that carpet the pond's floor, where they evaporate and materialize like magic. I'm certain the aquatic weeds help account for the large numbers of fish, because the pond, probably twelve feet at its deepest, doesn't seem deep enough to protect them from predators, and I doubt there are any rock formations to shelter them. Perhaps what I like most about Birch Pond is that you can often see the fish when they chase or strike your fly.

As I said, my first time out I didn't do well. I began the next time with a small, #10 Woolly Bugger, all black. Immediately a couple of fish nipped at it, but that was all. On occasion I could see fish chasing my fly but, again, that was all. I must have tried a dozen or so different flies, nymphs, flymphs, wet flies, dry flies, terrestrials, nothing. Hours passed unnoticed. Dusk was setting in. A devil's halo of gnats had formed around my head. Time to go home.

There are few things that can drive you more crazy than seeing trout rising all around and failing to get any of them to grab your lure. But I was undeterred. The next afternoon I was back at it, starting first with the woolly bugger, then trying fly after fly to no avail. I've found that when a fly is successful, it's successful right away, or at least with the first half dozen or so casts, so there's no need to keep failing the same fly for a long time. I'm sure there are exceptions to this maxim, such as the weather or time of day changing to make a particular fly more attractive, but generally speaking, there's no sense in being stubborn. If a fly isn't working, go to a new one. I tried lots of new on day two. Eventually I stopped, decided to study hard what the fish were rising for and match the hatch.

I've never felt particularly skillful at matching the hatch, figuring out what particular insect the fish were going for, but it seemed there was no other option. There were different insects floating on the pond, some flying up, hovering for a while, then landing back down again. But eventually I noticed that the most common one was a dark grey thing, quite small of course. Now I carry several fly boxes in my jacket, and all kinds of flies, and, in truth, I don't know all their names. I found something that looked most like the little emergers I thought the trout might be rising for, and cast a couple of times, letting the fly sit on the pond, then jerking it slightly on occasion. A trout soon struck, and as I reeled it in, I stepped back into the gap of the dock. The sensation was like walking into a room and suddenly finding a step down where you expect a level floor. I didn't get hurt, but I lost the fish. The holes in the dock were an extra challenge. I had another one on, but lost that fish also. My halo returned. I was hungry. It was time to go home.

Day three I was looking out over the pond. Dragonflies were striking the surface violently, probably eating the same insects the trout were rising for. There were swarms of magnificent darning needles, damselflies of a glittering blue weaving back and forth over the pond, their wings nearly invisible. A light breeze was making white sheets over the water and I was casting well, using the wind as my ally. I like to cast with a soft wind at my back. The added strength makes the fly go farther and drop more naturally. This wind was shifting directions across the pond, so I changed directions with it. Maybe I wasn't catching any fish, but at least I was casting nicely.

This day the fish were not rising for the same emergers as yesterday, and I couldn't have matched anything if my life depended on it. I found a dry fly that had a reddish head and tail, a brown back, iridescent green sides. I'd used the fly successfully in a creek that morning, landing two small brookies with it, so I figured the big brookies in Birch Pond would also like this fly. But I was apprehensive. This fly was a gem, my only one of its kind; I didn't know its name and was afraid of losing it before I could identify it in a book or a fly shop. I considered how reluctant fly tyers get hooked into tying their own.

Sure enough, twice fish went for it, and I had good fights, but these wild fish were able to twist away before I could land them. Through the translucent water I got a fairly decent look at the streaking fish. They didn't look like brookies. My fear of losing this special fly and failing to match it in the future won out. I figured I'd better quit using the fly, as it seemed inevitable that a fish was going to run away with it. (I later learned the fly is called a Flashback Hare's Ear, and it remains one of my all time favorites.) Nothing else that day worked. A big dragonfly

163

landed on my vest, near my shoulder. He did not want to leave. I looked closely at him. He began to move his jaws. In the insect world these jaws are enormous. He seemed benevolent. Trouble is, I just don't speak dragonfly.

Day four I brought the fly to a neighbor who makes superb flies, dropped it off with his wife who doesn't care much to know the names of flies, and asked her to ask him to make a half dozen for me. In the meantime, she let me buy some new flies. In June I've felt my luckiest patterns are Black Ants, Light Cahills, and the Fly Formerly Known as Prince. My neighbor doesn't make the Fly Formerly Known as Prince, but he does make Prince Nymphs, which are pretty much the same, but less gaudy. I bought several to experiment with, and Lola and I hiked back to the pond.

All three days of fishing on the pond were interesting in that each of the days had rain, lots of it, but I was never caught in any storms. I was lucky. The sun came out long enough for us to hike and fish, and the rain never resumed until Lola, who I now trusted to roam freely while I fished, and I reached the truck for home. Day four was no different. I went through the retinue of flies I'd bought that morning: a Green Drake, Cinnamon Ant, Shushan Postmaster, and finally, the Prince Nymph. From one side of the dock I was able to see fish chasing it, but no bites. I tried a couple other casts on the other side where fish had just risen and dropped the fly near the swirls the vanished fish had left behind. It didn't take long. My rod arced and I stripped some line to make sure the trout was well hooked, and tried to keep calm, stripping and reeling. I could see the fish streaking madly back and forth. Eventually I landed him. I was so excited I nearly fell off the dock. He was over a foot long, a brown trout. I've always felt browns were misnamed. The fish was golden, speckled with black and red spots that made the gold even more stunning. Trout, even of the same species, always appear different in different streams. Their colors and patterns seem to be affected by their diet and the waters they dwell in. I unhooked him quickly. He flopped back into the pond with no help.

How strange that browns were in this pond. Perhaps somehow they migrated here, but more likely, someone, probably long ago, had stocked them. The brown I caught, and suspect all his huge family, was well-finned and wild. Generations of browns had lived in this pond. When I was ready to cast again, the tippet line broke on my backcast, or maybe into the pond. I never found the line or fly. The fish had exhausted it. Just a second or two more, and he'd have snapped the line before I could have landed him.

A final observation concerning fishing for wild browns in this unusual high mountain habitat: Out of whimsy, frustration, a willingness to experiment, or simple desperation, I discovered that at times a salt water fly is highly effective, a small green imitation of some alien thing from outer space called a Comet.

Late Summer

In late summer the soft greens of spring turn richly dark. Along Camden Creek are clusters of wild aster and golden rod, purple and yellow. Surely this is not paradise, but might be a simulacrum of paradise, which raises the question, "Is there fly fishing in heaven?" All fly anglers know the answer to that question. So much so that to ask it is absurd. I sometimes like to think that this world is a rehearsal for the next, that what we experience in this world carries over into the next, and to live joylessly in this world is a squandered life. I find it impossible to believe that you can live a fulfilling life without a strong connection to the natural world. But how do you do that? Possibly paying attention to the details of nature, which fly fishing can make you do. Thoreau on his deathbed when asked about the afterlife, replied, "One world at a time." I, too, have nothing to offer regarding the next world, if one, or many, exist. It could be we simply merge into the universe, or we wake on another shore somewhere, where of course there are fish.

Pilgrimage

Actually, what I have written about Furnace Brook hasn't been about Furnace Brook at all. Instead, it has been about the many "Furnace Brooks" that are largely neglected by the fishermen who live closest to them. They need not be trout streams. They can be bass ponds, pickerel bogs, pike waters, catfish holes, panfish hotspots and opportunity in other guises.

The Philosophical Fisherman, Harold Blaisdell

It's a sunny Friday in August and I am journeying to Harold Blaisdell's local trout stream, Furnace Brook in Pittsford, Vermont, about an hour's drive from my house. I am doing precisely what Blaisdell admonished all anglers to avoid, ignoring my own nearby local stream, White Creek, which sometimes teems with wild squaretails, and foolishly driving far out of my local range to fish a stream I've merely read about that is hard to find on a map. Why am I doing this? The Mettawee, Indian, and Battenkill are all near my home, much shorter drives. Camden Creek is a short drive away. I can walk or ride my bike to Black Creek and White Creek, yet here I am, on my way to a brook in central Vermont that few fly fishers, if any, care about. To compound the foolish, Blaisdell in his book makes clear (or unclear) that he may not have been writing about the trout stream within sight of his home. Nevertheless, I love his book so much, and feel as though I love the man also, that I feel a strong pull to fish for brookies, which are most always small, in the stream he praised so much. Maybe I am just making sure the magic I feel in the places I fish is no lesser than the magic of the places Blaisdell praised. Maybe it's obsessive-compulsive, the need to see, to be there, even though I already know.

I drive around Pittstown a bit, a charming Vermont small town like so many others, with clear views of the Green Mountains most everywhere you look, but I can't find Furnace Brook, so I stop at the town's municipal center where the recreation director (seeming pleased I want to fish in Furnace Brook) gives me a town map and points me in the right direction. I see a covered bridge on the map, and find it easily. Covered bridges are excellent because there are often fish under the bridges and, even better, there is always a place to pull over and park.

167

The brook is crisscrossed with deadfall; it looks healthy with pools and currents; the banks are thick with greenery. There's very little litter, and no evidence of anyone having fished there, ever. I believe it's safe to imagine that the brook overall isn't much different from what it appeared like in the fifties and sixties when Blaisdell fished it. One spot in particular holds my interest. Right at the corner of the bank is an enormous sycamore that I guess to be 200 years old. It has three trunks, one of which, still alive, has fallen into the brook. Woody debris has gathered up against the tree, and in the pool behind the tree are young-of-the-year (born this past spring) brookies.

In a current upriver from the sycamore, I catch a six-inch chub, silver-scaled and white-bellied. What else I caught in Furnace Brook, I won't say. I was simply glad to see that there are still wild brookies in the brook, that some things don't change much, that there are still few people who fish there, and no one seems to pay any attention to anyone who does. I cannot help but suspect, however, that fifty years ago there were more fish in that brook, though I fished in only a tiny portion of it and am in no way informed enough to judge.

I have quoted frequently from Harold Blaisdell's book, possibly too much, but his work so frequently validated what I instinctively knew, that I felt the need to fish a brook he wrote about near his home. So, going against my own better judgment, I decided to fish in a place where many of his ideas took shape. Many years ago I did something similar by visiting Walden Pond. The beauty of that visit is that I realized that Walden is just another pond, or, actually, another lake. We ourselves participate in making a pond or lake or brook magical by bringing our own magic, or realizing the numinous quality of place by simply settling down, opening up, paying attention.

Perhaps sometimes we need to re-experience what we already know. The visit to Furnace Brook in no way demystified the stream, but reinforced my understanding that there are multitudes of fine trout streams all around, brooks where no one fishes, that sustain wild fish that I hope will be present long after I am gone, and that others with the need for wildness, solitude, and challenge can discover around the bend, not halfway around the world.

One Rainbow

There is a small stream near my home where I believe no one else ever fishes. This stream has wild rainbows. I usually wait until August to fish there. I often see anglers out casting their lines in April and May, but it's been my experience that most trout don't bite here in the Northeast until later in the summer. This is especially true when it comes to rainbow trout. I have no explanation for this except that rainbows possibly like the water a bit warmer than browns and squaretails, and I do not buy into the probability that I'm not doing things right, because I've tried many different methods in early spring.

One particular summer, late July or early August, I visited this stream. I was over-anxious, always a condition for failure. I passed by pools I was familiar with and saw no fish in them. I wandered well downstream, over and under deadfall, finding what appeared to one vacant pool after another. Puzzled, disappointed, I began making my way back to my truck when, in a particularly excellent pool where I'd frequently had success catching rainbows about a foot long (for me, with my one ounce rod, a lunker) I spooked dozens of fish. Why hadn't I seen them when I passed before? Was it the different angle of the sun, or had I scared them into hiding before I could see them? This pool is superb. It's deep and transparent, located at a bend in the river. A current runs into it, not too fast, not too slow. It has ledges and rocks for trout to hide, and a healthy sycamore hangs over it. Because it's around a bend, I can hide behind reeds while I cast, about 15 or 20 feet from the pool.

So I waited a while behind the reeds, selected a new fly, a nymph pattern, giving the fish time to emerge from hiding. Trout started rising in the pool for a hatch perhaps, too tiny for me to make out. Also, a fish rose behind me from a current not far upriver that had a log nearby. I straight away realized two things: one, I had been in too much of a hurry previously; two, I wasn't using the right fly. I tried about eight dry flies, one after another, but couldn't get the rising fish to go for mine. Switching to terrestrials, I tried a Black Ant, then a Floating Beetle. Nothing. I tried a tiny brown thing the name of which I still don't know. That almost worked. Finally a trout grabbed for it, but missed, then tired of it. I tried a Prince Nymph. Failure. I was thinking about trying a beadhead nymph but opted for a Gold-ribbed Hare's Ear, possibly a #14 or #16. The first cast nothing happened. The second, nothing. I made a good cast on the third try, just under the shade of the sycamore where the current brought the fly to approximately the center of the pool.

The fish lunged for it and I knew I had him. But then the line went slack, which is not unusual because often the struggling trout will swim toward you momentarily. The rainbow began leaping, three, maybe four times. I got him near the sandy bank as calmly as I could, but fairly quickly. I set my rod down in the reeds, lifted the fish from the water where I was easily able to free the hook from the side of his jaw. He vanished in a flash. That was enough fishing for me. I returned beaming to my truck, even though I'd caught only one, even though the rainbow was probably only nine inches long.

I don't know if this would have been enough to please other anglers. I was happy because the summer day was sweet and breezy. I'd a good fight with a stunning wild rainbow and, perhaps most of all, my persistence had worked.

Fishing in September

I love to fish the small streams in September. The light is softer, the breezes are balmy, the streams cool, gentle. Butterflies, monarchs, and sulfurs float along the banks casting their small shadows over the water. Sometimes a darting kingfisher startles me. The fall leaves have not yet covered the streams, and in the northeast there are still plenty of fish. There are difficulties, however. Every month's fishing is different, and if by September you've not grown weary of fishing, there are certain factors to keep in mind. We seem to get droughts now every August, so the water is often low, though the rains have picked up a bit by September. Many of the trout have retreated to deeper pools where a light current drifts into them. These are pools that were easier to fish earlier in the spring and summer when the water was higher and the riffs were stronger, making it harder for the fish to see your fly line and more easily fooled by your lure. The fish that remain in September are the survivors, the finicky ones that are much more reluctant to take a fly.

Many fly anglers will switch over to lighter tippets as the season grows later, from the standard 5X to 6, 7, 8, even 9X. For the uninitiated, X rating is a way of specifying the diameter of the tippet line in fractions of an inch. $0X = 0.011$ of an inch, $1X = 0.010$ of an inch, $2X = 0.009$, and so on. Therefore, the higher the number, the finer the line. But the finer the line, the more vulnerable it is to breakage. Some fishers switch over to tinier and tinier flies. I find this tiresome. Tinier flies are harder to knot on your line. Terrestrials? They will sometimes work, and I find them very effective later in the season, when insect life is still flourishing. I also believe that trout are less likely to bite when they are spawning, and browns spawn in September. But there is a special thrill in catching a wild trout late in the season, or even landing a holdover stocked trout late that has taken on habits of the wild. I've caught brookies into mid-October. Eventually the streams get covered in leaves and it becomes almost impossible to fish. What I've concluded is that the harder the fish get to catch in the fall, the closer we come to season's end. There comes a time when you have to call it quits, hunker down for the winter, and wait for spring.

The Last Day

Late October, still warm, but with the soft heat one feels in the fall sunlight, the kind of heat that is no longer vast as in summer, but shrinking, the cold not far off, my last day out. I knew I had something big on by the strength of the tug. I stripped line to set the hook, then began reeling quickly, the fish taking the line close to where I stood, then suddenly back out again toward the center of the pool. The line went slack momentarily as he moved in toward me again, but I knew the fish was still on. When you lose a fish the feel is different. There is a sudden loss of signal, of life on the line, an abrupt vacancy. I felt no such thing. All this happened within seconds, but when a fine fighting trout is on, time bends like your fly rod, and seconds, though sharp, seem to expand. Back in the center of the pool, maybe fifteen feet from where I stood in the current before it ran into the pool, the rainbow breeched, flailing his twisting, radiant body. He hadn't just leapt out of the water. He rocketed. For an instant he was suspended in mid-air, arcing at least ten feet, and I saw him flick his head, breaking the line before he plunged back into the wet.

It's tempting to claim he was two feet long. He was powerful and pulsing with life. My guess is that sixteen inches and several pounds would be more accurate. I had a good look at him. The thrill remains with me through the cold and the winter. I'll try for him again next year. Maybe he, or a sister or brother, will also fly from out of the green and into the airy blue. The experience is never quite the same. The thrill is always intense, and not renewed, but new, as breathtaking as the first time.

Eight Haiku

landed two rainbows
raised briefly
to the sky

heron, without words
tells where
fish hide

from the pool's womb
shimmering trout

streaking star—
trout taking fly

Higgs-boson—
elusive trout

infinitesimal satellite
in search of life—Green Grail

black ghosts or shadows
flee my shadow…
haunted brook

to catch a shooting star—
rod line lure luck

ABOUT THE AUTHOR:

When he is not fishing, Stuart Bartow teaches writing and literature at SUNY Adirondack and is also chair of the Battenkill Conservancy.

His most recent book of poems, **Questions for the Sphinx**, received the 2011 best book People's Choice Award from the Adirondack Center for Writing. He lives near the Vermont-New York border.

CPSIA information can be obtained at www.ICGtesting.com
Printed in the USA
LVOW06s1816171215

467025LV00002B/487/P

9 781312 564299